The Vicarious, Sacrificial, Atoning Death of Jesus Christ

The Vicarious, Sacrificial, Atoning Death of Jesus Christ

How We Benefit from the Death of Jesus Christ

Fr. Steven Scherrer, ThD

iUniverse, Inc.
New York   Bloomington

The Vicarious, Sacrificial, Atoning Death of Jesus Christ
How We Benefit from the Death of Jesus Christ

iUniverse books may be ordered through booksellers or by contacting:
iUniverse
1663 Liberty Drive
Bloomington, IN 47403
www.iuniverse.com
1-800-Authors (1-800-288-4677)

ISBN: 978-1-4502-2406-2 (pbk)
ISBN: 978-1-4502-2407-9 (ebk)
ISBN: 978-1-4502-2408-6 (hbk)

Library of Congress Control Number: 2010904985

Printed in the United States of America
iUniverse rev. date: 5/19/10

Contents

Introduction

The Vicarious, Sacrificial, Atoning Death of Jesus Christ is a collection of my essays and sermons on the theme of Christ's atoning death on the cross. It is a collection of biblical reflections on this central mystery of the Christian faith. I seek to look at this mystery from many different scripturally based points of view and reflect on the various aspects of this central mystery. My primary question throughout is this: *How is it that Christ's death on the cross saves us from sin and restores us to intimacy with God?* This work is, therefore, a prolonged meditation on this mystery.

The fundamental point of this book is that Jesus, on the cross, bore for us our punishment for sin, thus freeing us from this punishment and restoring us to union with God.

Considering that this is a collection of sermons that were originally written for new audiences, it necessarily involves repetition. Since each sermon had to be a complete unit in itself, it had to restate points already made in other sermons for other audiences and then try to reinforce, illuminate, and reflect further on these same central points in new ways.

I also believe that all good preaching is repetitious. We need to hear again and again in new and fresh ways the central and most important truths of our faith. A preacher who does not repeat is not a good preacher, for he does not know his audience's need for repetition. Another advantage of this method is that it keeps our attention focused on the one central mystery of Jesus Christ's saving death and its significance for us. I do not make an important point and then leave it to go on to consider other matters. Rather, I circle around this fundamental point of our faith again and again, trying to look at it afresh from ever new angles, as we do in meditation, in order to savor its beauty and penetrate its depth.

Christ's death on the cross brought us salvation. It saves us from sin, guilt, and eternal death and restores us to friendship and intimacy with God. It gives us forgiveness and peace of heart.

The Church needs to be renewed in our day by fresh contact with the biblical roots of this central mystery of our faith. If you are uncertain about the meaning of Christ's saving death, you will be a weak Christian. What you need to strengthen you in your faith is fresh biblical reflection on this central mystery. I offer this work as a contribution to this end.

The meaning of Jesus's saving death has interested me ever since my undergraduate college seminary years. During the past three years, though, I had time to investigate this matter more thoroughly, working through the books listed in the bibliography. I saw this as a double problem that involves: (1) a fresh understanding of the Trinity, and (2) the theology of the atonement.

I approached this topic with the following questions: (1) How do the Father and the Son relate to each other within the Trinity itself? (2) How can the Son propitiate the Father through his death on the cross? (3) Does this propitiation consist in the Son pleasing his Father through the loving gift of himself to the Father in sacrifice unto death on the cross? or (4) does it consist in the Son bearing the penalty for our sins by dying on the cross, thus satisfying divine justice? or (5) does this propitiation involve both of these elements?

As I proceeded with my investigation, further questions surfaced: (1) Was Christ's atoning work only a forensic declaration that we are just, or does it truly make us just? (2) What is the connection between the atonement and Christ's resurrection? (3) How do the sacraments of reconciliation and the Eucharist fit into this? and (4) how does the Eastern Orthodox understanding of divinization relate to the Pauline theology of justification?

A key breakthrough came for me when reading *The God of Jesus Christ* (Kasper 1986). In reading that book, I saw that although the Father and the Son have only one divine mind and one divine will between them, each person nonetheless possesses this common mind and common will in his own way, so each can relate to the other in knowledge and love as one distinct person to another. So, I saw that the atonement can fit into a proper understanding of the Trinity, namely that the sacrificial death of the Son on the cross could have a propitiatory effect on the Father in behalf of our salvation.

Reading *Romans* (Schreiner, 1998), *One with God: Salvation as Deification and Justification* (Kärkkäinen, 2004), and *Christ Present in Faith: Luther's View of Justification* (Mannermaa, 2005), I saw that the effect of the atonement was more than just a forensic declaration that we are justified—it was a *real* justification on the part of God, received by faith.

I then reflected further on the importance of the sacraments of the Eucharist and reconciliation for the transformation that Christ's death works in the Christian.

Finally, I became interested in the importance of good works and obedience to the will of God as essential to our further growth in holiness once we have been justified through our faith by Christ's death on the cross.

Concerning my earlier questions, I concluded that Christ's atoning work on the cross is a loving, sacrificial self-offering of the Son to his Father, which infinitely pleased the Father on our behalf, as well as a satisfaction of divine justice through Christ's bearing and suffering our penalty in place of us on the cross.

Throughout this investigation, I was writing sermons and posting them on my website (www.DailyBiblicalSermons.com), and these questions became the subject matter of many of these sermons. *The Vicarious, Sacrificial, Atoning Death of Jesus Christ* is an edited collection of some of these sermons and essays that are relevant to this investigation. I offer it as a contribution toward a deeper understanding and appreciation of the meaning of the sacrificial, propitiatory, atoning death of Jesus Christ on the cross for our salvation.

Scripture citations are from the Revised Standard Version unless otherwise noted.

Fr. Steven Scherrer
Ossining, New York

Part I:
Christ's Atoning Death:
The Basic Principles

Christ Our Savior—an Overview

The sin of Adam caused a break in our relationship with God. As Adam's descendants, we no longer inherit what he lost, namely his original intimacy with God. Because of his sin, we have become mortal and are born in a state of spiritual death. To reconcile us with himself, God revealed himself in the Old Testament. Abraham was justified by his faith that in his offspring all the nations of the earth would be blessed (Gal. 3:16; Gen. 13:15). The Old Testament saints were justified, as we are, through their faith in this descendant of Abraham. God therefore forgave their sins through their faith, just as he forgives our sins through our faith in his Son, who died for us on the cross. The death of the only Son of God paid our debt of suffering, due in punishment for our sins, so that we would not have to suffer it but could go free. God, who is all-merciful but also all-just, devised this way of forgiving us, and it is consistent with his nature as God. In showing forth his perfect mercy, he does not violate his perfect justice. But in acting in such a just way, he is supremely merciful, for he himself, in the person of his Son, suffers the just penalty due for our sins so that he, in all justice, and without violating his own perfect, divine justice, might most mercifully forgive us.

As a substitute for us, the Father sent the Son to suffer vicariously our punishment. He suffered alienation from his Father on the cross, becoming a curse for us (Gal. 3:13), crying out in anguish from the cross, "My God, my God, why hast thou forsaken me?" (Mark 15:34). He suffered this abandonment so that we would not have to suffer eternal death and this anguish of alienation from God, this spiritual death for our sins. He suffered it for us so we would not have to suffer it again. The penalty was paid but once by Jesus Christ on the cross for all the elect, for all those who believe in him. His dignity as God's only Son gave infinite value to his suffering, which he underwent in our place.

Yet God has only one nature, and there is but one God, one divine being. So it is not as though God cruelly sent another being, separate from himself, down to earth to suffer for us. Rather, he came himself in the person of his Son. The Father and the Son are distinct persons. Each addresses the other as "thou." However, they are but one being, sharing the same divine mind and the same divine will, each in his own way, whether as Father, Son, or Holy Spirit. In addition, Jesus also had his own human mind and human will as part of his human soul and human nature; but there is but one God, with only one divine mind and one divine will. So God himself really suffered our penalty for us on the cross in the person of the Son.

In order for the Son of God, who existed from all eternity in the bosom of the Father, to die for us, he first had to become man in the incarnation. This act of incarnation was itself a part of our salvation, for in Jesus Christ, God and man became one. In the incarnation, a human nature with a human mind and a human will was united to a divine person, the eternal Son of God, with his divine nature, containing his divine mind and divine will, which he shared with the Father and the Holy Spirit. Thus Jesus Christ provided a divinizing contact point for the human race to touch God in the flesh here on earth.

Jesus then died, paying our debt, which we could not pay, and rose to new life so that once our debt had been paid, we, through our faith in him, might rise with him to a new life in his resurrection. But before he died, he sacramentalized his body for us in the Eucharist so it could be extended in space and time … so we might continue to offer him in sacrifice to the Father in the Eucharist. Then we eat his sacramentalized body and blood in Holy Communion to take into ourselves Christ's eucharistic, human body, which contains his divine person with its divine nature. We eat his body and drink his blood so that his divine person and nature may enter our bodies and spirits and unite us to

God by sacramental, physical contact with Jesus Christ. Thus the very mystery of his incarnation—via the Eucharist—unites us to God. Once redeemed by his death, which paid our debt, the incarnate Christ thus becomes our sacramental and physical contact point with God, and we are divinized and grow further in holiness by coming into contact with him in the Eucharist.

The Eucharist is also our perfect worship of the Father. With all our love and devotion in the celebration of the Eucharist, we offer Christ to the Father, together with Christ's offering of himself to his Father. Christ offers himself to his Father in love and self-donation, in praise and adoration, sacrificing himself on the cross in the bond of the Holy Spirit. But he gave us the Eucharist so we could take part in the offering of this one sacrifice, which gained our redemption. The Eucharist makes us present at Calvary at the very moment of his perfect sacrifice so we might offer it with him to the Father and offer ourselves with him to our common Father, in the Holy Spirit.

The sacrifice of Christ is also a gift of love, a gift of self that the Son makes to the Father, thereby gaining eternal redemption for us. It thus becomes our perfect act of worship too, the sacrifice of the New Testament, which Jesus Christ has left to his Church as our perfect cult and worship of the Father in, through, and with Christ, in the unity of the Holy Spirit. The Eucharist is therefore the sacrifice that has won our redemption since it makes present the sacrifice of Christ who substituted for us on the cross, paying for us our punishment for our sins. It is also our own supreme act of worship, for it makes Christ's sacrifice present for us to offer with him in love to his Father.

The animal sacrifices for sins (see Lev. 16:4), which God gave to Israel in the Old Testament, prepared her to understand this, for in them the sinner placed his hand on the head of the victim, thereby transferring his sins to the animal (Lev. 16:21; 4:4), and then slew the animal, whose death vicariously substituted for him, the sinner. Thus an innocent victim bore the sin of the guilty, suffering his punishment in his place.

St. Paul teaches us that an animal does *not* have the power to take away sins (Heb. 10:4), but rather sins were forgiven through these sacrifices in a sacramental way, in that the animal represented the one and only truly effective sacrifice of the Son of God, and so God forgave them in advance when they offered these sacrifices in faith, for he knew that full and proper expiation would be made in the future by the death of his only Son on the cross, which these sacrifices represented for the people.

In all this, though, we should not make the mistake of thinking that it was only after the sacrifice of Christ that God was transformed from being the wrathful Lord of the Old Testament into the loving Father of the New Testament. It was the eternally loving Father who took the initiative in the first place, sending his only Son to die for us (Rom. 8:32). This was God's plan to forgive us by sending his Son to suffer our punishment for us, in our place, so that in forgiving us, he could be not only infinitely merciful but also infinitely just. The just penalty was thus paid, and the all-just God, most mercifully suffering the penalty himself, forgives us our sins in all justice and in all mercy.

Therefore, we are justified through our faith—that is, rendered and actually *made* righteous through the sacrifice of Jesus Christ on the cross. It is *God* who *makes* us righteous through the sacrifice of Christ; and if it is *God* who makes us righteous, then we *are* righteous *indeed*, for God's actions are effective. We receive this justification through faith. God therefore not only *declares* us to be righteous but actually *makes* us righteous since his declarations are effective. Thus our justification through believing in Jesus Christ is also, in itself, the first step of our sanctification, which is a progressive, lifelong growth in holiness with which we must cooperate.

Through our faith in Christ—especially via the sacraments—we are *made truly* resplendent and righteous in God's sight, and we begin our growth in further holiness through our lives of faith, prayer, obedience, and good works. We do not justify ourselves through our works. Only God justifies us and begins to sanctify us when we believe, but then, by the cooperation of our good works, we continue to grow in holiness.

The sacraments of reconciliation (Matt. 18:18; John 20:21–23) and the Eucharist are key in all of this. It is they that make this justification a *true, experiential reality* in the believer. That is why the Catholic tradition has always spoken of our justification in Christ as *true* justification, not merely a forensic *declaration* of justification that leaves us as we were before. Christ *truly* justifies us through his death on the cross when we invoke the merits of his death in faith, especially in the sacrament of reconciliation. It is then that this justification becomes a true, experiential reality in our lives, and we know and feel that we have *truly* been justified and made new. The Eucharist, then, continues to accompany and nourish us in our process of further growth in holiness.

The Atonement within a Personalist Trinitarian Context

Statement of the Problem

The doctrine of the atonement is difficult for many to understand and accept, and some have rejected it in the sense that Jesus's death on the cross is a sacrificial and propitiatory death by which he gains for us the remission of our sins and the gift of eternal life.

I think, though, that many could be helped to understand better and accept this doctrine if they were to look at it in a more personalist way (as persons in relation) and within a Trinitarian context, also interpreted along more personalist lines, i.e., as persons in relation. In theological circles today, there is great interest in examining the Trinity afresh along personalist lines, seeing it in a more dynamic way (see Ware).

There Is but One Mind and One Will Shared by the Three Persons of the Trinity

In the past, the Trinity was studied in a way that often did not so strongly highlight the interpersonal dynamics and relations between the divine persons. This is partly due to the stress placed on the one common divine nature of the three persons, and due to the fact that the divine mind and the divine will pertain to the common divine nature, so that the three persons have but one mind and one will between them.

Since the will is the faculty by which we love, and the mind is the faculty by which we understand ourselves as persons distinct from others and able to relate to them, it was hard to see how the three divine persons could experience themselves as individuals, conscious of themselves as individuals, in relationship to the other two persons, and how they could love each other if they have but one mind and one will, shared among the three of them.

That they do have but one mind and one will between them, which pertains to their common nature, and not to their persons, is clear from the fact that Christ, who was a divine but not a human person, had both a human mind and a human will, as well as a divine mind and a divine will. But if he "had" no human person, to what then did his human mind and human will pertain—except to his human nature. That Christ was also a human person was condemned as the heresy of Nestorianism in 431 by the Council of Ephesus. The same must then also be true of his divine mind and divine will. They must in like manner also pertain to his divine nature rather than to his divine person.

But if this is true of Jesus, then it must also be true of the other two persons of the Blessed Trinity. In other words, their divine mind and divine will must also, in a similar way, pertain to their divine nature, not to their persons. But in God there is but one nature. Hence there is but one divine mind and one divine will to be shared by all three persons of the Blessed Trinity.

So this is the problem we are faced with today. It is easy to understand with this schema how the Trinity is a unity—having but one mind and one will—but it is not so easy to see how the three persons can interact and interrelate with each other in a conscious, personal, and loving way if between them there is but a single divine mind and a single divine will, which pertain to their common nature and in which all three persons share.

Toward a Solution to the Problem

The Economic Trinity as Persons in Relation

Yet when we turn to the scriptures, we see that the three divine persons know, love, interrelate with, and influence each other. Jesus prays, for example, to his Father, saying, "Father, I desire that they also, whom thou hast given me, may be with me where I am, to behold my glory which thou hast given me, for thou hast loved me *before* the foundation of the world" (John 17:24). We see in this scripture that Jesus can talk to his Father, and that the Father and the Son both knew and loved each other *before* the incarnation, "before the foundation of the world" (John 17:24), that is, before Jesus had his own human mind and human will, distinct from his divine mind and divine will. So we see that Jesus's communicating with the Father is not just limited to the time of his incarnation on earth, during which time he does have a human mind and a human will that are distinct from his divine mind and his divine will that he shares with his Father. But here in John 17:24, it is clear that it is the divine person of Jesus who is speaking, saying that he existed from all eternity, and that the Father loved him before he had a human mind and a human will, that he loved him, in fact, before the creation of the world, and that was certainly before the incarnation.

So how is it that the Father knew and loved the Son from all eternity if they had but one divine mind and one divine will between them? Cardinal Walter Kasper has written as follows on this problem, saying, "It is impossible to accept three consciousnesses in God ... We may say that the one divine consciousness subsists in a triple mode ... This means that a triple ... subject of the one consciousness must be accepted and at the same time, that the three subjects cannot be simply unconscious but are conscious of themselves by means of the one consciousness ... We have no choice, then, but to say that in the Trinity, we are dealing with three subjects who are reciprocally conscious of each other by reason of *one* and the *same* consciousness which the three subjects 'possess,' each in his own proper way" (Kasper, 288–289). The divine persons, Kasper continues, are thus "infinitely more dialogical than human persons are," and in God "there is also an infinitely greater interrelationality and interpersonality than in human inter-personal relations" (Kasper, 290).

This seems to me to be the proper solution to this problem, namely that in virtue of the one divine consciousness, the three divine persons are three distinct subjects, each conscious of the other and capable of loving the other, for each one possesses the one consciousness in his own distinct way.

Hence in the Trinity, we are dealing with persons in relation, persons in the relationship of love, even though the divine persons are not persons in exactly the same way that we are persons, as separate individuals with our own independent minds and wills. In God, the three persons form but one single being, and they are intimately united, one in mind and will. They are more perfectly united than man and wife in a perfect marriage, where they are one in mind, will, and heart.

In fact, in this more dynamic and personalist understanding of the Trinity, we can see better how the Son is even capable of offering himself in sacrifice to the Father, as to a distinct divine person—not to a distinct divine being but to a distinct divine person—who can then pour out upon him still another divine person, the Holy Spirit, filling the Son with the Spirit of the Father's love.

This is what happens on the cross, but when it is put into this Trinitarian context, we can immediately see that the death of Christ on the cross only carries out in a more dramatic fashion and within a human nature the basic Trinitarian pattern that has been going on from all eternity within the Trinity.

The Persons of the Trinity Are Distinguished from Each Other Only by Their Relations

To understand the above, we need to make another point first, namely that what distinguishes the divine persons from each other is not their essence or nature, which they all hold in common as all being equally God, but rather, as theologians have always pointed out, their *relations* one to another. The Father is distinguished from the Son only in that he is Father and has a paternal relation to his Son. And the Son is distinguished from the Father only in that he is a son and has a loving, filial relationship with his Father.

The Trinitarian Relations are Eternal, Not Just Limited to the Time of the Incarnation

Everyone recognizes this Father-Son/paternal-filial relationship during the time of the incarnation in which Jesus is subject and obedient to his Father, but the key to a deeper Trinitarian understanding of the doctrine of the atonement is to realize that this loving filial relationship of obedience, submission, subordination, and worship, on the part of the Son vis-à-vis his Father, is not just something limited to his earthly life; rather, it is an eternal Trinitarian relation that the Son has always had and always will have with the Father.

The Son was sent by the Father into the world. But if he was sent by the Father into the world, this means that this took place before the incarnation, and so we see that the relationship of the Father to the Son in eternity before the incarnation was one of a father with authority over an obedient son, who accepts his mission from the Father and becomes incarnate in the world. This relationship of sending and being sent is an authority-submission, paternal-filial relationship in which the Son, while one in essence with the Father and thus equal with him in divinity, is nonetheless sent by the Father and is obedient to him. Bruce Ware (Ware, 76–83) points out clearly that we are here dealing with an eternal Father-Son relationship, an eternally subordinate relationship of the Son to his Father, although in divinity the two are equal. The Son's subordination is not in his essence or nature, in which he is the same as his Father, but in his relation to his Father as Son. His relation to the Father is that of an obedient, subordinate, submissive, adoring Son. And this was eternally the case, not just while Jesus was a man on earth.

We see this throughout St. John's gospel, where Jesus is said to be sent by the Father, for example: "For God so loved the world that he gave his only Son, that whoever believes in him should not perish but have eternal life. For God sent the Son into the world, not to condemn the world, but that the world might be saved thorough him" (John 3:16–17). If the Son was *sent* into the world by the Father, then this happened before the incarnation, and therefore the paternal/obedient filial relationship of father to son also existed before the incarnation. We see this in many passages, such as the following: "do you say of him whom the Father consecrated and sent into the world, 'You are blaspheming,' because I said, 'I am the Son of God'?" (John 10:36), or "For I have come down from heaven, not to do my own will, but the will of him who sent me" (John 6:38). These quotations could be multiplied many times over, but they are sufficient to show that this relationship of an obedient, submissive, subordinate son to his father extends back from all eternity, long before the incarnation of the Son. It is not just something concerning Jesus as a man in his humanity being submissive to his Father. He has always related in this way to his Father, who even before his incarnation sent him into the world.

This relationship of submission, subordination, obedience, and adoration on the part of the eternal Son from all eternity toward his Father also extends in the other direction as well, namely into the infinite future, as Ware points out (Ware, 83–85). We see this clearly in the fact that Jesus is exalted after the resurrection to the right hand of the Father (Heb. 10:12), a position of glory but also of subordination to the Father, who himself is seated on the throne. It is also clearly seen in 1 Corinthians 15:28: "When all things are subjected to him, then the Son himself will also be subjected to him who put all things under him, that God may be everything to every one." This will be in the future, when the Son will subject all things to himself, and then subject himself to the Father.

Therefore, if this relationship of subordination and submission as a son to his father is eternal—past, present, and future—it is part of the interior dynamics of the immanent Trinity from all eternity and forever.

With these clarifications, we are now able to put the death of Jesus on the cross into this personalist Trinitarian context.

The Eternal Pattern of Jesus's Sacrifice on the Cross within the Immanent Trinity

Jesus's death on the cross was a unique event in the life of the Trinity, for on the cross the Son offered himself within a human nature to the Father in love and self-gift. Yet this pattern of acting on the part of the Son toward his Father has been going on for a long time, long before Jesus was born in Bethlehem; in fact, it has been going on from all eternity. Here is where we can fit the doctrine of the atonement—more personally interpreted—into the doctrine of the Trinitarian relations, likewise interpreted along more personalist lines.

We should, then, understand that the Son, who always existed in a submissive, subordinate, loving, and filial relationship with his Father from all eternity and unto all eternity, has always been offering himself to his Father according to the pattern in which he offered himself to his Father on the cross.

First of all, he was always a Son, and the Father always had a Son. And so he always existed in relation to his Father as a son, filially, submissively, obediently, subordinately, adoringly, and lovingly, as a perfect son to a perfect father, equal to the Father in his *essence* as God, yet subordinate to him in his *relation* as Son. It is precisely this eternal filial *relation* that constitutes him as a distinct person from the Father, that constitutes him as the Son, for all the rest he holds in common with the Father.

The Son's subordination and filial submission to his Father was not just the result of the incarnation. He was not just subordinate as a man during his human lifetime on earth, but rather his subordination is from all eternity, just as he is eternally the Son, eternally relating in a filial way to his Father, who is also eternally his Father, eternally relating in a paternal way to his Son in love, as a perfect, loving father to a perfect, loving son; and as a perfect, loving son to a perfect, loving father.

The Son always related like this, in this perfect filial way toward his Father, as a perfect son in love, adoration, obedience, and perfect submission and subordination to his father, even though he was fully equal to his Father in divinity because he had the same essence and nature as his Father.

So, what Jesus did in incarnate form on the cross is what he has always been doing from all eternity in a non-incarnate way in the interpersonal, intratrinitarian relationships of the eternal immanent Trinity—he has always been offering himself to the Father in perfect filial love and submission, in obedience and adoration, as a perfect son to a perfect father in a perfect son-father relationship.

If there is anything at all that we can say with certainty about the persons of the Trinity, it is that they are relational. Theologians tell us that the divine persons are pure relation—"subsistent relations"—pure relation of father to son, and of son to father; pure filial relation of son to father, and pure paternal relation of father to son. And the relation itself, which glues them together in perfect love, is relationality, namely the Holy Spirit, the Spirit of their relation of mutual love.

The Father was always infinitely pleased by this self-offering in filial self-gift of love of his only-begotten Son. And as a result, the Father has always been pouring out upon his beloved Son the Spirit of his own divine love, that is, the Holy Spirit, which covered the Son with splendor and glory. So the Son has always been living in the splendor of the Father. The Son, in turn, has always been returning this same loving breath of the Holy Spirit to his Father.

Understanding the Atonement
within a Personalist Trinitarian Context

But then—and here is where the atonement is fully interpreted in personalist terms and within a Trinitarian context—in the fullness of time, the Father, in his love, sent the Son to become incarnate in human flesh. So now in human flesh, the Son continues this same eternal pattern of relating to his Father as he has always done in love and self-oblation, but this time there is a difference. This time, he can offer himself as a true sacrifice unto death because now, for the first time possessing a mortal human nature, he can suffer and die, which he does on the cross, following the same pattern of loving self-donation whereby he has always related to his Father and has always offered himself and pleased him in doing so.

As a result, the Father is so pleased—infinitely pleased—that he, as usual, pours out upon his Son his Holy Spirit, which this time raises him from the dead; and then, through the Son, he breathes out this same Holy Spirit upon all who share a common human nature with the beloved Son if only they believe in the Son.

The New Testament Witness to the Atonement

We are now, I believe, in a good position to better understand and accept the New Testament witness to the doctrine of the atonement, namely that Jesus's death was a sacrificial (Mark 10:45; Heb. 9:12, 14, 26, 28; 10:10, 12, 14), propitiatory (Rom. 3:25; 1 John 2:2; 4:10; Heb. 2:17) death that intercedes (Rom. 8:34; Heb. 7:25; 9:24: 1 John 2:1) for us with the Father, thereby gaining for us the gift of the messianic outpouring of the Holy Spirit, the renewal of the human race, and the gift of eternal salvation.

The Son Propitiates the Father for Us

St. John says, "We have an advocate (*paraklēton*) with the Father, Jesus Christ the righteous; and he is the propitiation (*hilasmos*) for our sins, and not for ours only but also for the sins of whole world" (1 John 2:1–2). As our advocate with the Father, the Son intercedes for us, which means that he propitiates the Father on our behalf. Propitiation is the normal meaning of the Greek word *hilasmos*, which means to render someone favorable toward us. We have someone who appears for us before the Father to propitiate him on our behalf. "In this is love, not that we loved God but that he loved us and sent his Son to be the propitiation (*hilasmon*) for our sins" (1 John 4:10). The Father took the initiative, but nonetheless the Son cooperated and carried it through to completion. Jesus was therefore our high priest before the Father to propitiate him for our sins, as Hebrews says: "Therefore he had to be made like his brethren in every respect, so that he might become a merciful and faithful high priest in the service of God, to make propitiation (*hilaskesthai*) for the sins of the people" (Heb. 2:17). "To make propitiation" or "to render favorable" is the ordinary Greek sense of the verb here. And, of course, there is the most important text of all, Romans 3:25, about Jesus Christ, "whom God put forward as a propitiation (*hilastērion*) by his blood, to be received by faith. This was to show God's righteousness, because in his divine forbearance he had passed over former sins." Again the Father takes the initiative in sending the Son to do this in human flesh, and this demonstrates God's righteousness because the divine Son pays the price for the forgiveness of former sins. God is hence just, as well as merciful, in forgiving our sins.

The Son Intercedes with the Father for Us

Hence we have an intercessor eternally before the Father, eternally interceding for us. Therefore, St. Paul asks, "Who is to condemn? Is it Christ Jesus, who died, yes, who was raised from the dead, who is at the right hand of God, who indeed intercedes (*entygchanei*) for us? "

(Rom. 8:34). How does Christ make intercession for us before the Father? He does so by the loving gift of himself unto death, within a human nature, in propitiatory sacrifice to the Father, which infinitely pleases the Father on behalf of all who share a common human nature with the Son and who believe in the Son. This is how he is our intercessor before the Father. He is our "advocate" (*paraklēton*) before the Father (1 John 2:1). He is also our advocate before the Father in that he has borne our penalty for us on the cross, and so can plead that we should now therefore be acquitted of any further punishment.

The Letter to the Hebrews also speaks explicitly of Christ's intercession. It says about Christ that "he is able for all time to save those who draw near to God through him, since he always lives to make intercession for them" (*eis to entygchanein hyper autōn*) (Heb. 7:25). We note that he will always be doing this for us. And again about intercession, Hebrews says, "For Christ has entered, not into a sanctuary made with hands, a copy of the true one, but into heaven itself, now to appear in the presence of God on our behalf" (*nyn emphanisthēnai tō prosōpō tou theou hyper ēmōn*) (Heb. 9:24). What is he doing appearing in God's presence for us? He is interceding for us. How? Through the merits of his loving self-offering unto his Father in sacrificial death, as well as through his substituting for us on the cross, vicariously bearing our suffering for us in punishment for our sins. This is how he *intercedes* for us, propitiating the Father on our behalf.

The Son Sacrifices Himself to the Father for the Remission of Our Sins

Christ's death is a sacrifice that takes away our sins, as the Letter to the Hebrews makes clear in many statements. For example, Hebrews says that Christ entered not an earthly but a heavenly tabernacle, the heavens themselves, and not with the blood of animal sacrifices, but with his own blood for the sake of our redemption. It says, "He entered once for all into the Holy Place, taking not the blood of goats and calves but his own blood, thus securing an eternal redemption"

(Heb. 9:12). "How much more shall the blood of Christ," Hebrews says, "who through the eternal Spirit offered himself without blemish to God, purify your conscience from dead works to serve the living God?" (Heb. 9:14). Therefore, Christ's blood, offered in sacrifice on the cross and now brought into the heavenly sanctuary, cleanses our consciences. It infinitely pleases the Father on our behalf, in that Christ lovingly offered himself even unto death in love to the Father for us and bore our penalty on the cross for our sins.

The effect of all this is to take away our sins by the sacrifice of himself once for all on the cross, as Hebrews says: "But as it is, he has appeared once for all at the end of the age to put away sin by the sacrifice of himself" (Heb. 9:26). His single sacrifice took away the sins of many: "So Christ, having been offered once to bear the sins of many" (Heb. 9:28). Indeed, we have been made holy by Christ's doing his Father's will and offering himself up, as Hebrews says, "And by that will we have been sanctified through the offering of the body of Jesus Christ once for all" (Heb. 10:10). That is what he did, and so now he sits in glory: "But when Christ had offered for all time a single sacrifice for sins, he sat down at the right hand of God" (Heb. 10:12). Let our final quotation be this conclusive one: "For by a single offering he has perfected for all time those who are sanctified" (Heb. 10:14).

Conclusion

I think that we are now in a much better position to understand and accept this New Testament witness to the sacrificial, propitiatory, intercessory, and atoning death of Jesus Christ on the Cross. The doctrine of the Trinity, understood in a more personalist way, greatly illuminates the traditional doctrine of the atonement. Christ has reconciled us with the Father—at the Father's initiative—by his loving self-offering on the cross, and by his substituting for us on the cross, vicariously bearing in our place the suffering due to us in punishment for our sins so that we could go free.

God Suffers Our Punishment

"He who did not spare his own Son but gave him up for us all "
(Rom. 8:32)

I

The Trinity is the mystery that the Father, the Son, and the Holy Spirit are all three equally God, equal in divinity. Jesus therefore said, "Go therefore and make disciples of all nations, baptizing them in the name of the Father and of the Son and of the Holy Spirit" (Matt. 28:19).

All three are persons, but they are not like human persons, with each being a separate and different being. These three divine persons, on the contrary, have but a, single being between them: a single substance; a single essence; a single nature that they all share. All these latter terms mean basically the same thing. Yet these three persons relate to each other as distinct persons. Both the Father and the Son address each other as "thou," each relating to the other as a separate person, distinct from himself, to whom he can speak. The Father, furthermore, can and does send the Son into the world; but the Son, being a son in a subordinate relationship of a son to his father—although equal in essence and therefore in divinity with his Father—does not send the Father. For the salvation of the world, the Father sent the Son to become man so that he would be able to suffer as a man on the cross to save us from our sins. His death satisfied divine justice and the righteous wrath of the Father against our sins because the Son paid in our place, by his death on the cross, the debt of suffering due to us in punishment for our sins.

We cannot say that it was unjust or cruel of the Father to send his Son and afflict him in this way with our sins and punishment, for the

Son is but one being—a single substance—with the Father. The Son (as are also the Father and the Holy Spirit) is the one and only God. Therefore the one and only God suffered our punishment for us, to be able to *justly* forgive us, for it is necessary that God be just. Someone must suffer in order for justice to be done, and that someone must be of sufficient dignity to satisfy divine justice. That person is the Son of God himself. Hence God himself is the one who, in the person of his Son, suffers the just penalty for our sins so that we can justly go free, for the penalty has been justly and fully paid.

This is important for us, for knowing that our forgiveness has been justly given gives peace to our consciences, for in this way, we know that we have been truly forgiven, that the slate is now cleared, the debt paid, and the case properly and justly closed. It is not just a free "presidential pardon." A real price has been paid—the just price—for our forgiveness to be justly given. It gives us great satisfaction and inner peace to know this.

Because it is God himself, in the person of the Son, who suffered our punishment for us to save us, this act of salvation is both infinitely *just* and infinitely *merciful*. What could be more merciful than God himself suffering our punishment for us so we would not have to suffer it and could therefore go free? And what could be more just than God requiring that such a high price be paid for our sins? Yet this way is much more merciful and much more just than if God were simply to forgive us gratuitously without regard to justice and the need that the debt for sin be paid. So God came himself, in the person of his Son, and bore the burden of our sins himself in his death on the cross, thus freeing all who believe in Jesus Christ from eternal death and from the burden of sin and guilt.

II

It is a great wonder, as I have already noted, that in God there is but one single mind and one single will pertaining to the one nature of God; and that each of the three persons shares in this one divine mind and one divine will. Yet each divine person possesses this one mind and one will according to his own mode, that is, as Father or as Son or as Holy Spirit. In addition, Jesus Christ also had a human mind and a human will, distinct from his divine mind and divine will, but perfectly united to and submissive to his divine mind and divine will, which he shared in common with the Father and the Holy Spirit.

Mind and will pertain to the nature, not to the person. This can be clearly seen in the case of Jesus Christ, as I have already pointed out, since he had but one person and two natures. His one person was divine. Of his two natures, one was divine, the other was human. Therefore, his human mind and human will have to pertain to his human nature since he had no human person to which they could pertain. In the same way, then, his divine mind and divine will must pertain to his divine nature, rather than to his divine person.

But if the divine mind and divine will of Jesus Christ pertain to his divine *nature*, and not to his divine *person*, then the divine mind and divine will of the Father and of the Holy Spirit must also pertain to their divine *nature*, and not to their *persons*. But in God there is only *one* nature, which all three persons possess in common. So if the divine mind and divine will pertain to this one common *nature*, and not to each of the three individual *persons*, then it is clear that each of the three persons shares in this common divine mind and common divine will, for they share this one, common divine nature between them. Hence it is clear that in God there is only *one* divine mind and *one* divine will, shared in by all three persons, although each person possesses this one divine mind and one divine will, each in his own way, as Father or as Son or as Holy Spirit. God can therefore be addressed as "thou," as we so often do in our prayers, as to *one* being, with but *one* mind and *one* will.

Therefore when the Father sent the Son into the world for our salvation, there was but one divine mind and one divine will operating in this mission, although each person was using this common mind and common will, each according to his own mode, as Father or as Son or as Holy Spirit. Therefore, in sending his Son to die for our sins, God was not being cruel; rather, he came himself to bear our sins in the person of the Son.

Christ Substituted for Us on the Cross

"Yet it pleased the Lord to bruise him; he hath put him to grief; when thou shalt make his soul an offering for sin, he shall see his seed."
(Isa. 53:10 King James Version, KJV)

Jesus died to save us from sin and from the just wrath of God against the sin of Adam and against our own sins (Rom. 1:18). God himself took the initiative in sending his Son to propitiate his own righteous and necessary wrath against human sin. A just God can only be wrathful in the face of sin; and sin, in all justice, must be punished by an all-just God.

When, however, we speak of "wrath" in terms of God, we must purify our concept from what we as human beings usually understand and experience as wrath. Our wrath is human and imperfect. We often lose control of our emotions and are carried away by them. None of this is true of God. In God, wrath simply means the strong, divine reaction against all moral evil.

The Father took the initiative and sent us his own Son to properly propitiate his own righteous and necessary divine wrath by suffering the just penalty for our sins so that God in his perfect justice might remain perfectly just, and yet not exact from us the punishment for which we ought to pay. Jesus's death satisfies the righteous and necessary divine wrath against our sins because it pays our debt of suffering in punishment for our sins so that we, in all justice, might be set free.

This act of propitiation by the death of Jesus is at the same time supremely merciful because it is God himself, in the person of his own Son, who suffers this punishment for us, freeing us from having to suffer it. God is one. There is only one God. The Son is one being with the Father, one single God with him, although a distinct and different person within the Godhead. Hence it is God himself who comes to suffer for us, and in our place, the just penalty for our sins so that he, the just God, can in all justice let us go free since our debt has been paid. He himself paid it! Therefore, the Father is in no way being cruel in sending his Son to suffer in our place, as though he were sending another being, separate from himself, to suffer in order to satisfy and placate his own wrath. God comes himself. His Son is not a separate being—although a distinct person—from himself.

Many places in the scriptures speak of the wrath of God. For example, this beautiful Christmas psalm is full of divine wrath: "Thou didst withdraw all thy wrath; thou didst turn from thy hot anger. Restore us again, O God of our salvation, and put away thy indignation toward us! Wilt thou be angry with us for ever? Wilt thou prolong thy anger to all generations?" (Ps. 85:3–5).

The death of Jesus, then, truly propitiates the divine wrath, in that it satisfies it; that is, it satisfies justice, a just price has been paid for our sins, and God can therefore justly forgive them and let us go free. The righteous wrath of God is therefore turned aside, propitiated, and God is reconciled with us. God himself has done this to reconcile himself with us. God himself satisfies his own righteous wrath in this way, so that he might forgive us in the only way appropriate to God: justly.

But does this picture of a wrathful God contradict our picture of a loving God? Not at all! God was always a loving God. There is never any question about that. Jesus does not transform a wrathful Lord into a loving Father. God was always a loving Father, even in his wrath against our sins. It was his great love that moved him in the first place to devise this method of saving us—at such great expense to himself—from his own necessary wrath, namely by suffering it himself instead of inflicting it on us. The sending of Jesus to suffer in our place is the plan of an ever-loving Father, who is also a just God, and who will not violate his own justice in order to show mercy. The death of Jesus on the cross is the way he did it.

Justice is part of God's nature. It is not merely some external law that God has to obey. God himself *is* just. He is justice itself. He is also love itself and mercy itself. This is God's nature, and he always acts according to his nature, in a just, loving, and merciful way. The propitiatory death of Jesus Christ on the cross is the way a just and merciful God has devised to forgive us for our sins and yet at the same time remain a fully just, loving, and merciful God—all three at the same time—without one attribute violating the other.

The propitiatory death of Jesus Christ on the cross shows that God is just, even though he forgives and justifies us through our faith without demanding any further just punishment from us (Rom. 3:25–26). Without the death of Christ paying our debt of punishment, God would indeed seem unjust in letting us off without inflicting on us the just and proper punishment. God does not give us a mere "presidential pardon." A just penalty *is* paid, and paid in full, and a very high penalty at that, the highest possible penalty, the death of the Son of God, who is God himself! In other words, God himself paid his own penalty for us. The sacrifice of Christ, therefore, shows that God is indeed just, even though he justifies and forgives without imposing the death penalty on us, which we deserve (Rom. 3:25–26).

The death of Jesus on the cross then is far more than merely an example of love. It is true propitiation and true expiation of our sins in the blood of Jesus Christ on the cross. It is not just an example of Jesus's love and forgiveness, in that he forgave even those who crucified him. It is far more than that. It is real propitiation of the real divine wrath. It is God himself, in the Son, suffering his *own* wrath, to satisfy its just demands. God himself takes the initiative to propitiate his own divine wrath by sending his Son to die on the cross, in our place, so the just penalty for our sins might be fully paid.

This is the great gospel message, namely the sacrificial, propitiatory, atoning death of Jesus Christ on the cross. The proclamation of the death and resurrection of Jesus Christ is the kerygma of the Church, the joyful good news, that through faith in Christ, we are forgiven and saved from the just wrath and punishment of God, due to us for our sins, and will henceforth have a new life in the risen Christ. This is the joyful proclamation that God sent his own Son to substitute for us and to suffer instead of us, in place of us, the punishment due to us for our sins, thus bringing to an end his just wrath against us and in this way reconciling himself to us. We receive this liberation from punishment and guilt by means of our faith and through the sacraments that make us clean and resplendent before God, clothing us in the splendor of the righteousness of Jesus Christ himself (Isa. 61:10).

"It pleased the Lord to bruise him; he hath put him to grief" (Isa. 53:10 KJV). Hence it was God himself who smote his own Son, inflicting on him the punishment due to us for our sins, in order to free us from this punishment and guilt. The debt of our punishment, once paid, is then removed from us. This is the gospel of salvation, which God has sent into the world in his Son. Christ justifies us through our faith in him when we invoke the merits of his death for us on the cross. He took our place. He substituted for us. God smote him instead of smiting us. "It pleased the Lord to bruise him; he hath put him to grief" (Isa. 53:10 KJV), "and with his stripes we are healed" (Isa. 53:5 KJV), made new, a new creation (2 Cor. 5:17), new creatures, new men in Jesus Christ, our Lord (Eph. 4:22–24).

The suffering of Christ to pay our debt is effective and frees our consciences from guilt because we realize and see clearly that our just penalty has indeed, in all justice, been paid for us. When the merits of the blood of Christ are individually and personally applied to our wounded and guilty hearts in the sacrament of reconciliation (Matt. 18:18; John 20:21–23), we really do feel forgiven and know for certain that our guilt has been removed, and that we are truly made (not just declared) just and righteous in God's sight and in reality by his death on the cross for us.

God then raised Christ from the dead to manifest that his sacrifice in substitution for us was accepted. Hence the resurrection manifests that we are truly justified and illumines us with new light. St. Paul therefore says that Jesus Christ "was put to death for our trespasses and raised for our justification" (Rom. 4:25). That is, the resurrection manifests the justification achieved by his death.

"And the Lord hath laid on him the iniquity of us all" (Isa. 53:6 KJV). "But he was wounded for our transgressions, he was bruised for our iniquities; the *chastisement* of our *peace* was upon him; and with his stripes we are healed" (Isa. 53:5 KJV). In his justice, God bruised him and put him to grief (Isa. 53:10 KJV), thus punishing all sin. But he did so with great mercy, for it was God himself, in the person of his Son, who suffered this punishment for us, to free us from it and thus forgive us for our sins, that we might rejoice in the freedom of the sons of God (Rom. 8:21).

What Christ Suffered for Us

"But one of the soldiers pierced his side with a spear,
and at once there came out blood and water."
(John 19:34)

The soldier pierced Jesus's side with a spear to verify that he was dead. But why did water also come out, not just blood? Could this be an indication that he was not only dead, but that his heart literally broke physically from what he suffered spiritually, psychologically, and emotionally on the cross?

And what did he suffer? He suffered the hatred of those whom he had come to save. But the martyrs also suffered the hatred of their enemies, and yet many of them suffered this with joy and courage, such as St. Ignatius of Antioch, who longed and thirsted for martyrdom, and begged the Romans not to intervene on his behalf to commute his sentence of death. But Jesus, on the contrary, had great fear before he suffered, and he asked his Father that his cup of suffering might be removed from him (Luke 22:42); and in his agony before his death "his sweat became like great drops of blood falling down upon the ground" (Luke 22:44). Jesus also cried out from the cross, "My God, my God, why hast thou forsaken me?" (Mark 15:34). How different was the death of Jesus from that of so many martyrs—like St. Ignatius of Antioch—who went to their deaths with joy and great desire to die for Christ. How different was Jesus's death from that of St. Polycarp, for example, who died in silence as he was burned alive! What, then, did Jesus suffer in his heart that was more than these others suffered? What was it that made his death so much more terrible than theirs?

The answer is that he suffered the wrath of God for our sins. God himself smote, chastised, and abandoned Jesus on the cross (Isa. 53:10) so that he might suffer in his heart the divine wrath, which all sinners deserve, in order to free them from this great suffering of heart. He experienced in his heart the frown of God upon all the sins of the world, the abandonment of God, alienation from God, and the depression of hell; and he suffered this in our place, instead of us, so we would not have to suffer this agony and alienation from God for our sins, as we otherwise would have suffered it. He suffered God's terrible wrath on the cross, feeling forsaken by God, so we might live in the happiness of God and even die in happiness, as did so many martyrs.

Jesus Christ was smitten and wounded by God in his human heart. This was his greatest suffering, being alienated from God in his heart. "He was wounded for our transgressions, he was bruised for our iniquities: the *chastisement* of our *peace* was upon him; and with his stripes we are healed … and the Lord hath laid on him the iniquity of us all" (Isa. 53:5–6 KJV). Jesus Christ was even cursed by God (Gal. 3:13) in being hung from a tree (Deut. 21:23); and in being cursed in place of us, he "redeemed us from the curse of the law," which is death (Gal. 3:13). Yes, he suffered even this for us, the curse of God! Jesus suffered the abandonment of his Father on the cross in order to absorb the divine wrath for us, to free us from it.

Indeed, now we see how his death was more terrible than the deaths of all the martyrs.

Justified by Faith

"Knowing that a man is not justified by works of the law but
through faith in Jesus Christ, even we believe in Christ Jesus, in
order to be justified by faith in Christ, and not by works of the law,
because by works of the law shall no one be justified."
(Gal. 2:16)

Here, we are presented with the fundamental doctrine that God justifies us, that is, makes us righteous, not by means of our own good works according to the law, but as a free gift through the merits of the death of Jesus Christ on the cross for all who believe in him and invoke his name with faith. We can then grow further in holiness by cooperating with the grace of God through obeying his will and living a life of good works. Good works, therefore, show forth the faith of those who have been justified by Christ through their faith.

St. Paul did not want to have his own righteousness, earned by his own good works, but rather the splendid righteousness of God, which is far more glorious and marvelous, and to be clothed with this splendor through his faith in Jesus Christ. He says that he wants to "be found in him [Christ] not having a righteousness of my own based on law, but that which is through faith in Christ, the righteousness from God that depends on faith" (Phil. 3:9).

The splendid righteousness of God on the one hand, and merely human righteousness on the other hand, cannot be compared. Even a person who is perfect in the human righteousness of the law through his own good works and personal effort—if there ever were such a person, and St. Paul tells us that there has never been such a person (Gal. 2:16; Rom. 3:20)—would be nothing in comparison with a person who is justified through his faith in Christ and filled with the splendor of the righteousness of Jesus Christ himself. Even St. Paul, who "as to righteousness under the law [was] blameless" (Phil. 3:6), now that he has discovered the far better and far more glorious righteousness of God in Jesus Christ, says, "Whatever gain I had, I counted as loss for the sake of Christ" (Phil. 3:7). He only wants to be found in Christ, not having a righteousness of his own based on law, "but that which is through faith in Christ, the righteousness from God that depends on faith" (Phil. 3:9).

Isaiah prophesied this splendid righteousness of Christ, saying, "He has clothed me with the garments of salvation, he has covered me with the robe of righteousness" (Isa. 61:10). The truth is that "now the righteousness of God has been manifested apart from the law ... the righteousness of God through faith in Jesus Christ for all who believe ... they are justified by his grace as a gift, through the redemption which is in Christ Jesus, whom God put forward as a propitiation by his blood, to be received in faith. This was to show God's righteousness, because in his divine forbearance he had passed over former sins; it was to prove at the present time that he himself is righteous and that he justifies him who has faith in Jesus ... for we hold that a man is justified by faith apart from works of law" (Rom. 3:21–22, 24–26, 28).

In other words, "now the righteousness of God has been manifested apart from the law" (Rom. 3:21), in that Jesus Christ died on the cross instead of us, suffering himself our punishment for our sins, for our sake, and in our place, so that the price of our redemption having been justly paid by him, we might go free, acquitted and justified, that is, made righteous. He suffered our punishment for us, and so everything is just, and God is just—he has not violated his justice on our behalf. All is well and justly done and justly paid. Therefore, if we have faith in Jesus Christ, we are gratuitously justified "through the redemption which is in Christ Jesus" (Rom. 3:24). Truly, God put him "forward as a propitiation by his blood, to be received by faith. This was to show God's righteousness, because in his divine forbearance he had passed over former sins" (Rom. 3:25).

God might seem unrighteous in forgiving our sins without demanding a just punishment for them. This problem is solved by Christ bearing this just punishment. Therefore God now appears to be fully righteous in forgiving us, because the just penalty was fully paid for us by God, himself, in Christ. "This [act of atonement] was to show God's righteousness, because in his divine forbearance he had passed over former sins [without demanding a just punishment for them]. It [the atonement in Christ] was to prove at the present time that he himself is righteous and that he justifies him who has faith in Jesus" (Rom. 3:25–26). Not only does God prove his own righteousness in the death of Christ, but he also makes us righteous by that same death. The death of Christ "was to prove at the present time that he himself [God himself] is righteous and that he justifies him who has faith in Jesus" (Rom. 3:26).

"To one who does not work but trusts in him who justifies the ungodly, his faith is reckoned as righteousness" (Rom. 4:5). Our task is to believe in Christ for our justification, for "if righteousness comes through the law, then Christ died in vain" (Gal. 2:21 NKJV). Christ came into the world to be cursed by God, accepting to suffer the divine curse for our sins in place of us, "having become a curse for us—for it is written, Cursed be everyone who hangs on a tree" (Gal. 3:13; Deut. 21:23).

The tragedy of the Jews, on the other hand, is that, "being ignorant of the righteousness that comes from God, and seeking to establish their own, they did not submit to God's righteousness" (Rom. 10:3). Let us not follow their bad example, rejecting the gift of God because we prefer our own righteousness according to our own works in following the law.

Therefore, if you want to walk in the light (John 8:12; 12:46; Eph. 5:8; 1 Thess. 5:5), confess your sins, leave them behind, and believe in Jesus Christ to be justified by your faith in him and be clothed with his splendor, with his robe of righteousness (Isa. 61:10), being clothed with

Jesus Christ himself (Gal. 3:27; Rom. 13:14); and clothe yourself with the new man, created in Jesus Christ through faith (Eph. 4:22–24). Thus you will be a new creation (2 Cor. 5:17), for Christ came to make all things new (Rev. 21:5). In Christ "neither circumcision counts for anything, nor uncircumcision, but a new creation" (Gal. 6:15). Live, then, in the splendor of God by believing in Jesus Christ for your justification!

Christ Became a Curse for Us

"For all who rely on works of the law are under a curse; for it is
written, Cursed be every one who does not abide by all things
written in the book of the law and do them ... Christ redeemed us
from the curse of the law, having become a curse for us—for it is
written, Cursed is every one who hangs on a tree."
(Gal. 3:10, 13)

If we have not always obeyed all the laws of God, we are guilty and
under a curse for not having obeyed them. "Cursed be he who does
not confirm the words of this law by doing them," says Deuteronomy
(Deut. 27:26). And James says, "For whoever keeps the whole law but
fails in one point has become guilty of all of it" (James 2:10). St. Paul
says, "For all who rely on works of the law are under a curse; for it is
written, 'Cursed be everyone who does not abide by all things written
in the book of the law, and do them'" (Gal. 3:10: Deut. 27:26). Under
these conditions, we are all guilty, and all under the curse of God, for
none of us has kept all of the laws all of the time.

Who can free us from this guilt and this curse, which is the greatest
suffering we can have, the suffering of a guilty conscience for having
sinned. It is Christ who frees us from this curse by becoming himself
accursed instead of us and in place of us. He has borne our curse so that
we would not have to bear it. He has substituted for us. He became
accursed by being hanged on a tree, for the law says, "And if a man has
committed a crime punishable by death and he is put to death, and
you hang him on a tree, his body shall not remain all night upon the

tree, but you shall bury him the same day, for a hanged man is accursed by God; you shall not defile your land which the Lord your God gives you for an inheritance" (Deut. 21:22–23). And St. Paul says, "Christ redeemed us from the curse of the law, having become a curse for us— for it is written, 'Cursed be every one who hangs on a tree'" (Gal. 3:13; Deut. 21:23). Hence in being cursed in place of us, as our stand-in, our substitute, Christ has freed us from this curse of God.

We are all under a curse and are guilty because we have not observed well all the laws of God all the time. What we need, therefore, is God's mercy to forgive us, not his justice to justly condemn us. And God gives us his mercy through our faith in the death of his Son on the cross.

But this mercy and forgiveness come to us justly, for our just penalty was indeed duly suffered, in that Christ suffered the just punishment due to our sins for our sake. Thus all justice was fulfilled, and God did not violate his own justice in showing us his mercy.

Thus we are justly able to escape punishment for our sins and be freed from our guilt for committing them. What just mercy is this! This was the divine plan for forgiving us. And it works. Countless people have experienced its effectiveness in their lives. This forgiveness is at the same time both merciful and just. Precisely because it is just and because we know that it is just, it works and relieves our consciences of guilt and sets us free.

This is God's great solution to human guilt. Do you feel guilty for having sinned or for having fallen into some imperfection? God has a remedy for you that works: the death of his Son on the cross, invoked with faith. Invoke with faith the merits of his death on the cross for your sins, especially within the sacrament of reconciliation, which Jesus gave us for this purpose (John 20:23; Matt. 18:18), and God will free you from the pain caused by your guilt—and there is no worse pain than the pain of guilt.

The death of Christ on the cross, invoked with faith, is good medicine for your spirit and your heart. Come to him to be healed of the sickness and pain of your conscience, a sickness for which there is no human or medical remedy, a sickness which is the worst of all sicknesses! To heal this worst of all sicknesses, this great pain in your heart, is the reason that Christ came into the world. He came so we might rejoice in his presence.

The Law Upheld

"'My son, your sins are forgiven … But that you may know that the Son of man has authority on earth to forgive sins'—he said to the paralytic—'I say to you, rise, take up your pallet and go home.'"
(Mark 2:5, 10)

Our greatest problem is sin and the resultant guilt, which is a pain in our hearts, diminishing or destroying our peace and joy of spirit. We can endure illness with happiness and peace in the Lord, but who can endure depression of spirit for having sinned? As Proverbs says, "A man's spirit will endure sickness; but a broken spirit who can bear?" (Prov. 18:14). Nothing breaks the spirit as much as guilt for having sinned. Even the saints, who had long since stopped serious sinning, still suffered this pain of spirit on account of their imperfections. The saints were extremely sensitive and suffered anguish over the imperfections into which they continued to fall, as we see, for example, in the saintly desert fathers who wept over their sins.

This is why Jesus Christ was sent into the world, to be our Savior from sin and guilt—and this includes imperfections—so we might at last have a jubilant spirit before the Lord. He forgives our sins by offering himself to God as a gift, giving "himself up for us, a fragrant offering and sacrifice to God" (Eph. 5:2).

Jesus Christ is the means God used in order to forgive us for our sins, while at the same time still upholding his holy law, which requires that sins be justly punished. St. Paul, after saying that "a man is justified by faith apart from works of law" (Rom. 3:28), concludes by saying, "Do we then overthrow the law by this faith? By no means! On the contrary, we uphold the law" (Rom. 3:31). St. Paul's teaching upholds the law in the sense that the law demands death as the punishment for sin, and our sins are laid upon Jesus Christ (2 Cor. 5:21; Gal. 3:13; Isa. 53:6), who died on the cross to fulfill the law for us and in our place. Christ's death was then the death required by the law as the punishment for sin. So, in sending Christ to die for our sins, God upholds his law.

The law is upheld and fulfilled in the death of Christ on the cross. We are forgiven, and yet the law, which requires the punishment of death for sin, is not violated. In this way Christ is the means used by God to justly forgive our sins in accordance with the requirements of the law, upholding at the same time both his just law and his mercy. And we, through Jesus Christ, are assured that our sins, which depress our spirit, are forgiven, especially when we use the sacrament of reconciliation, which he gave us for this purpose (Matt. 18:18; John 20:23). Thus we are freed from sin to rejoice in the freedom of the children of God (Rom. 8:21).

Faith in Jesus Christ assures us that we are saved by the death of Christ on the cross from our sins and imperfections, which sadden and depress us. In being justified through faith, we are now no longer condemned. We no longer live under the condemnation of God, but rather our spirits are freed from the burden of guilt. "There is therefore now no condemnation for those who are in Christ Jesus" (Rom. 8:1), for God "condemned sin in the flesh, in order that the just requirement of the law might be fulfilled in us" (Rom. 8:3–4). That is, in sending his Son "for sin" (Rom. 8:3), or as a sacrifice "for sin," God "condemned sin in the flesh" of Jesus Christ on the cross (Rom. 8:3). Sin was thus condemned so we might not be condemned. Sin was condemned in the flesh of Jesus Christ, in that he suffered the penalty of the law against sin, thus fulfilling "the just requirement of the law" for us (Rom. 8:4). Christ "fulfilled" "the just requirement of the law" (Rom. 8:4) for us in his death. Hence he upheld the law by his death. Yet the law can no longer condemn us. Its just penalty has already been paid, and we are therefore freed, no longer condemned by the law or by God. In the death of Christ, the law is upheld and fulfilled, and we are freed and saved from its just penalty.

Christ Died to Fulfill the Law for Us

"Think not that I have come to abolish the law and the prophets; I have come not to abolish them but to fulfill them."
(Matt. 5:17)

The law of God, revealed through Moses, always has a place in the life of the new people of God. It reveals to us God's will, namely that we be holy, separated from the world, and worshipers of God, offering him sacrifice. Christ fulfilled the Mosaic Law.

St. Paul says, "All who rely on works of the law are under a curse; for it is written, Cursed be every one who does not abide by all things written in the book of the law, and do them" (Gal. 3:10; Deut. 27:26). And St. James says, "Whoever keeps the whole law but fails in one point has become guilty of all of it" (James 2:10).

It is good that we feel ourselves to be transgressors of the law, for so we are, and the law helps us to come to this awareness. Only when we come under conviction of sin and feel ourselves to be sinners, can we come to saving faith in Jesus Christ, who himself bore the curse of God for our sake by being hung on a tree (Gal. 3:13; Deut. 21:23). In other words, Christ bore this curse for us so we would no longer have to bear it.

Hence through our faith in Christ, we are no longer under the curse of God, no longer alienated from God by our sins. In this way, he redeemed us. He died in our place after being cursed by God. Thus through his redemptive death on the cross, we are reconstituted as righteous, Christ having fulfilled the just requirement of the law on our behalf for our sins, suffering its just curse and just punishment in our place.

Thus in this sense, the law has permanent meaning for the Christian. It shows us God's justice, which Christ fulfilled for us. Christ fulfilled the justice and the just requirement of the law for us. He died "in order that the just requirement of the law might be fulfilled in us" (Rom. 8:4).

The law, of course, also has a rich meaning for us in that the moral law—especially the Ten Commandments and all their implications—shows us how we are now to live as Christians once we have been justified by our faith, not by the works of the law. It shows us God's will for us, which we are to obey. We are justified by our faith, not by our works, not by our observance of the moral law, but the moral law has continued meaning for us, for it shows us how we are to sanctify ourselves by doing God's will. It shows us what God's will for us is so that we know what to do to sanctify ourselves. I note here that I am speaking of the Old Testament moral law, not of its ceremonial law.

Old Testament Preparation

"On the tenth day of this seventh month is the Day of Atonement; it shall be for you a time of holy convocation, and you shall afflict yourselves and present an offering by fire to the Lord. And you shall do no work on this same day; for it is a day of atonement for you before the Lord your God."
(Lev. 23:27–28)

The Day of Atonement is one of the most important holy days in Israel. Its details are explained in the sixteenth chapter of Leviticus. This celebration and the regular sin offerings of the Israelites are figures of Christ's atoning death. They prepared the Israelites, and us as well, to understand Christ's sacrificial, substitutionary, atoning death.

On the Day of Atonement, two male goats were offered in expiation for the sins of the people. One was slain and offered in the sanctuary, and his blood was sprinkled upon the mercy seat, that is, the propitiatory, or the cover of the Ark of the Covenant. The other male goat was not slain, but Aaron put his hands on his head and confessed over him the sins of the people, putting them upon the animal, who was then led out into the desert and let go, carrying away with him into the desert the sins of the people. Scripture says, "And Aaron shall lay both his hands upon the head of the live goat, and confess over him all the iniquities of the people of Israel, and all their transgressions, all their sins; and he shall put them upon the head of the goat, and send him away into the wilderness by the hand of a man who is in readiness. The goat shall bear all their iniquities upon him to a solitary land; and he shall let the goat go in the wilderness" (Lev. 16:21–22).

Here we see the practice of confessing and placing the sins of the people on an animal by putting their hands on his head and making this confession. In this particular case, the goat carried these sins away into the desert. In the usual sacrifices for sins, the sinner also placed his hand upon the animal's head but then killed him, while the priest sprinkled his blood in front of the veil of the sanctuary and put it also on the horns of the altar of incense (Lev. 4:4–7). The meaning is that the sins of the sinner are transferred from the sinner to the animal, who dies in vicarious punishment for the sinner, in his place, substituting for the sinner, thus paying the sinner's debt of suffering in punishment for his sins, and the sinner goes free, his due punishment having been justly paid for him by the animal.

In itself, as St. Paul teaches us (Heb. 10:4), the sacrificed animal does *not* have the power to take away sins, but rather functions sacramentally, in that the sacrificed animal represents the perfect sacrifice of Christ, which *does* have this power to substitute for us and endure the suffering due to us in punishment for our sins. So God gave the Israelites these sacrifices so that by confessing their sins over the head of the animal, placing their hand upon his head, their sins might be forgiven, not by the sacrifice of the animal, but by the sacrifice which the animal represents, namely the sacrifice of Jesus Christ, the only Son of God, on the cross.

The paschal lamb is another Old Testament type of Christ and his vicarious death for our salvation. The Israelites presented every firstborn, in memory of the blood of the paschal lamb sprinkled on their door posts, which saved them from the plague of the death of the firstborn (Exod. 12:12–13; 13:15). Thus the paschal lamb was a substitute for their own firstborns. The lamb was sacrificed and died instead of and in place of their firstborns when the holy and righteous wrath of God struck down the firstborns of the Egyptians.

Jesus Christ is the true Passover lamb, the fulfillment of this Old Testament type. He is "the Lamb of God who takes away the sin of the world" (John 1:29). He is the true paschal lamb, who dies instead of us, as a substitute for us, thus absorbing the just and holy wrath of God against our sins so that we might not die. Like the paschal lamb in Egypt, he died so we might be saved from the plague of death. He suffered the plague of death instead of and in place of us. His death saves us from the death sentence that we should have paid and would otherwise have had to pay.

Jesus is the true paschal lamb that died instead of us to save us from the plague of death. As the paschal lamb saved the firstborn of the Israelites, so Jesus, the Lamb of God, saves all who believe in him from the punishment of death for their sins, dying in their place, thus absorbing for them, the just wrath of God.

How It All Started

"And the Lord God commanded the man, saying, You may freely eat of every tree of the garden; but of the tree of the knowledge of good and evil you shall not eat, for in the day that you eat of it you shall die."
(Gen. 2:16–17)

In the beginning, God created Adam and Eve in a state of perfection, righteousness, and intimacy with God, and he created them immortal, "for God created man for incorruption, and made him in the image of his own eternity, but through the devil's envy death entered the world, and those who belong to his party experience it" (Wis. 2:23–24). God gave Adam a clear commandment not to eat of "the tree of the knowledge of good and evil" (Gen. 2:17). For having disobeyed this commandment, he would die—that is, become mortal and experience spiritual death. He thus lost his state of righteousness and intimacy with God and was cast out of the garden of Eden (Gen. 3:22–24).

Christ was sent into the world to restore us to a state of righteousness before God and to conquer death. The death of Christ on the cross destroyed our spiritual death—our separation and alienation from God—in that Christ himself underwent this suffering of alienation from his Father on the cross on our behalf, and in place of us, so that we would not have to suffer it. We then rise with Christ to a new life in his resurrection; and his resurrection is also the first fruits of the resurrection of our body on the last day, "For as in Adam all die, so also in Christ shall all be made alive" (1 Cor. 15:22).

Because of his sin, Adam lost his state of righteousness and intimacy with God; and his descendants would inherit only what Adam had to bequeath to them. God would send Jesus Christ so that through faith in him, we might recover our state of righteousness and intimacy with

45

God, being forgiven for our sins and clothed with the righteousness of Jesus Christ himself, "For as by one man's disobedience many were made sinners, so by one man's obedience many will be made righteous" (Rom. 5:19).

The disobedience of Adam, together with its negative consequences for us, is canceled out by the obedience of Jesus Christ. Christ obeyed by dying on the cross in place of us, thus accepting into himself our just punishment for our sins; and so by this just act of one single man, Christ, all those who believe in him are constituted righteous; just as by the unjust act of one single man, Adam, all are constituted sinners. "Then as one man's trespass led to condemnation for all men, so one man's act of righteousness leads to justification and life for all men" (Rom. 5:18).

He Made Him to Be Sin

"For our sake he made him to be sin who knew no sin, so that in him
we might become the righteousness of God."
(2 Cor. 5:21)

With this verse, we are at the very heart of the mystery of the atonement, which Christ worked for us on the cross. In himself, Christ was without sin, but for our sake God "made him to be sin" (2 Cor. 5:21)— that is, he laid our sins upon him. God did this so Christ might suffer for our sins their just punishment according to the law so we would not have to suffer it, but rather could go free, justly forgiven, being made righteous before God. Christ, carrying out sins, suffered their just punishment so that we would not have to suffer it. He was our substitute in undergoing for us the punishment we should have suffered for our sins. Therefore we can go free because Christ suffered our sentence for us.

St. Paul therefore says, "For our sake he made him to be sin who knew no sin, so that in him we might become the righteousness of God" (2 Cor. 5:21). "The Lord hath laid on him the iniquity of us all" (Isa. 53:6 KJV). Hence "the *chastisement* of our *peace* was upon him; and with his stripes we are healed" (Isa. 53:5 KJV). His "chastisement" brought us peace because he suffered instead of us for our sins. He was cursed by God instead of us for our sins, to free us from the curse of God (Gal. 3:13; Deut. 21:23).

According to the law, Christ was cursed by God, for he was hanged on a tree (Deut. 21:22–23). God took out his righteous wrath on him, and Jesus suffered it, in this way absorbing the wrath of God, which he has against all sin. Now we can go free, for there is no further wrath to absorb. Christ's death therefore sets us free from the wrath of God.

God, in "sending his own Son … for sin … condemned sin in the flesh, in order that the just requirement of the law might be fulfilled in us" (Rom. 8:3–4). In other words, God sent his Son as a sin offering, and thus he condemned sin in the flesh of Jesus Christ, in order to fulfill the just requirement of the law for us, who will therefore not have to fulfill it. The just requirement of the law was that sinners die for their sins. Jesus Christ fulfilled this just requirement of the law for us by dying on the cross. "There is therefore now no condemnation for those who are in Christ Jesus" (Rom. 8:1). We are, therefore, no longer condemned but are made righteous through our faith in Jesus Christ. "In him we… become the righteousness of God" (2 Cor. 5:21).

All Saved in the Same Way

"And he made no distinction between us and them, but cleansed
their hearts by faith."
(Acts 15:9)

In the first days of the Christian faith, the disciples discovered that the
salvation of God, sent into the world through the death and resurrection of Jesus Christ, was for everyone who believed, whether he was a
Jew or a Gentile. At first, though, they thought that only Jews could be
saved through faith in Christ. But seeing that the Gentiles received the
Holy Spirit and spoke in tongues (Acts 10:46), just as they themselves
did, they realized that it was not necessary that Gentiles first become
Jews, be circumcised, and keep the ceremonial law of the Jews.

This was a great and important discovery, for now Christianity could
truly become a universal, world religion for people of every nation who
believe in Christ. It was no longer limited only to Jews, or to those who
would first become Jews. St. Peter discovered this with Cornelius, and
St. Paul discovered it in his travels, for example, in Antioch in Pisidia,
where he preached to Gentiles. "And when the Gentiles heard this, they
were glad and glorified the word of God; and as many as were ordained
to eternal life believed" (Acts 13:48).

God has foreknown and ordained those who were to be saved by
invoking the name of his Son. All who truly believe in him are among
these blessed elect ones. How important is it then to preach his name
and salvation unto the ends of the earth (Mark 16:15; Matt. 28:19),
for this is the plan of God from all eternity for their salvation in Jesus
Christ. Through faith in his name, the elect will come to new life once

the gospel is effectively preached among them. This is God's predestined plan, that we preach Christ to the ends of the earth, to nonbelievers, and in this way the elect, planned by God from all eternity for salvation, will believe the gospel and be transformed by their faith in Christ. Our preaching of Christ and the people's response to it will make it clear who are God's elect.

We ourselves continue to be filled with wonder and amazement at this discovery. It is a marvel in our own lives as well. We see how the name of Jesus has the power to cleanse us of all guilt and give us the happiness of God, true happiness, which is the fruit of the Holy Spirit. And we obtain this happiness only by invoking with faith the name of Jesus Christ. It is he who heals our wounds and gives us a new heart, radiant with the love of God and happy in his service, with the burden and pain of our guilt and sin removed.

God purifies the hearts of all his elect in the same way, through their faith in Jesus Christ, dead for our transgressions and risen for our new life. Dying, he paid our debt; and rising, he illumined our life. Dying, he destroyed our death; and rising, he restored our life. Through his cross and resurrection, he renewed the world. So, "we believe that we shall be saved through the grace of the Lord Jesus" (Acts 15:11), all in the same way—Gentiles as well as Jews. "For there is no distinction between Jew and Greek," says St. Paul, "the same Lord is Lord of all and bestows his riches upon all who call upon him. For everyone who calls upon the name of the Lord will be saved" (Rom. 10:12–13). "And there is salvation in no one else, for there is no other name under heaven given among men by which we must be saved" (Acts 4:12).

All Salvation Is through Christ

"He that believeth on the Son hath everlasting life: and he that believeth not the Son shall not see life; but the wrath of God abideth on him."
(John 3:36 KJV)

The Son of God is our salvation from the righteous, just, necessary, and holy wrath of God against our sins. He was sent to us by the Father to save us from his own just, holy, and necessary wrath, for whoever does not believe in the Son, "the wrath of God abideth on him" (John 3:36 KJV). The Son was the means used by God to save us from his own wrath and forgive us instead of punishing us for our sins. Through the Son—through our faith in him—God could forgive us and at the same time punish our sins in the Son, instead of in us, for he was our substitute before the Father, and God did to him what he otherwise would have done to us. God's wrath does not have to be satisfied twice—once in his Son and then again in us—if we invoke the merits of Christ's death on the cross. Invoking Christ's merits on the cross causes them to be counted as our having suffered our just punishment. It is therefore important to believe in the Son and invoke the merits of his death if we want to be forgiven and reconciled with God.

In this way God gives us relief from the pain and depression caused by guilt. He also gives us jubilation of spirit in being reconciled with him. Our consciences also stop accusing us, giving us peace in our hearts. This state of peace with God through the forgiveness of our sins is the beginning of eternal life. In the Son, we have God's life in us, and we will live with him forever. This is what the gospel says: "He that believeth on the Son hath everlasting life" (John 3:36 KJV). St. John says in his first letter that "he who has the Son has life; he who has not the Son has not life" (1 John 5:12). In fact, if we believe in the Son, we "shall not come into condemnation," but rather have already "passed from death unto life" (John 5:24 KJV). Through faith, we have already begun our eternal life with Christ ahead of time in the midst of this old life.

The Old Testament saints also had the Son through faith and hope (John 8:56), and so, therefore, "Abraham believed God, and it was reckoned to him as righteousness" (Rom. 4:3; Gen. 15:6), as St. Paul says. He was justified by his faith, as we are.

St. Peter says before the council, "God exalted him at his right hand as Leader and Savior, to give repentance to Israel and forgiveness of sins. And we are witnesses of these things" (Acts 5:31–32). Forgiveness of sins only comes through the death and resurrection of Jesus Christ, for, as St. Peter says, "There is salvation in no one else, for there is no other name under heaven given among men by which we must be saved" (Acts 4:12). If pagans are saved (see the book of Jonah), it will be through their faith; and their salvation will come to them through the death on the cross of Jesus Christ and through his resurrection, even though they may not know this, as also Abraham did not know it.

It is nonetheless of supreme importance that Jesus Christ and his saving death on the cross and life-restoring resurrection be preached to "every creature" (Mark 16:15 KJV), unto the ends of the earth, and that we "make disciples of all nations, baptizing them in the name of the Father and of the Son and of the Holy Spirit" (Matt. 28:19), as the risen Christ told us, so that they might have now already in this life the assurance of their salvation in Christ, the relief of the forgiveness of their sins, and the joy of living with God in Jesus Christ, their Lord and Savior.

Born Again

"Verily, verily, I say unto thee, Except a man be born again, he
cannot see the kingdom of God"
(John 3:3 KJV)

Our faith in Jesus Christ *truly* transforms us, that is, Jesus Christ truly
transforms us through our faith in him. Our justification by faith, and
not by our own works, is accompanied by an interior regeneration of
our whole being when we believe in Jesus Christ. In other words, sanctification accompanies justification, with the result that in being justified by faith, we are also, at the same time, born again. Our rebirth
shows that our justification works a *real* change in us. God works a
bath of *regeneration* in us, as St. Paul affirms, saying that "Not by works
of righteousness which we have done, but according to his mercy he
saves us, by the washing of regeneration, and renewing of the Holy
Ghost" (Titus 3:5 KJV).

Our condition in Jesus Christ is totally new and different from
what it was before. We are now justified and sanctified, that is, we are
made truly new, really righteous, and holy, and placed in a long process of further growth in sanctification. We are also born again, that is,
regenerated. The change that God works in us is *real*. We are made a
new creation (2 Cor. 5:17; Gal. 6:15; Rev. 21:5) and new men (Eph.
4:22–24). Hence St. Paul says, "So you must also consider yourselves
dead to sin and alive to God in Christ Jesus" (Rom. 6:11).

Christ died to destroy our sins, to free us from depressing guilt and
eternal death, and to give us a new life without sin. He paid our debt
according to the law, and so we do not now have to pay it again, being
freed from the punishment due to our sins because he suffered it in our
place. He then rose from the dead so that we might rise with him to

new, regenerate, born-again lives in which we now seek the things that are above, and no longer those of the earth (Col. 3:1–2).

We die in his death to our sins, being freed from sin by his death, and we rise in his resurrection to walk in "newness of life" (Rom. 6:4), that is, to live a new, holy, justified, righteous, and born-again life. We are regenerate people in Jesus Christ.

If we were baptized as infants, we need to actualize our faith now as adults in order to activate our regeneration and thus begin to live a truly new life that is different from the life of those who do not believe in Christ. We are to avoid sin in order to be happy with God and live in his love, not under his wrath. But if we fall into an imperfection or sin, we can take refuge in his blood, poured out for us in sacrifice, in order to be forgiven and healed again, and so once again experience his love.

Christ is now calling us to be born again and born from above, to live a new life—a new kind of life—through our faith in him.

Made Truly Righteous

"And you, who once were estranged and hostile in mind, doing evil deeds, he has now reconciled in his body of flesh by his death, in order to present you holy and blameless and irreproachable before him."
(Col. 1:21–22)

This is the doctrine that we believe. This is the great gift that God has given us in his Son Jesus Christ. Christ reconciled us with God "in his body of flesh by his death" (Col. 1:22), and he did so that we might be "holy and blameless and irreproachable before him" (Col. 1:22). God reconciled the world to himself through his Son, "making peace by the blood of his cross" (Col. 1:20). The result of this reconciliation is that we are made "holy and blameless and irreproachable before him" (Col. 1:22).

We see here that the justification which God has given us in Jesus Christ is real, not fictitious. He *really* does make us righteous, holy, blameless, and irreproachable. He makes us resplendent before him by means of the blood of the cross and the death of his Son. "In him we have redemption through his blood" (Eph. 1:7). We would have died eternally in hell for our sins if Christ had not reconciled us with the Father through his blood. Christ "condemned sin in the flesh" (Rom. 8:3), that is, in his own flesh, by dying in our place to save us from the eternal death of hell. He did this for us "in order that the just requirement of the law might be fulfilled in us" (Rom. 8:4), and the justice of the law demands eternal death for our sins. He paid this debt for us by pouring out his blood on the cross, thus condemning sin in his flesh, reconciling us in his body of flesh through his death, and "making peace by the blood of his cross" (Col. 1:20). Thus he fulfilled the just requirement of the law for us (Rom. 8:4).

This justification is communicated to us through our faith in the Son of God, and especially through the sacraments of reconciliation and the Eucharist, which we are meant to use and experience regularly, the Eucharist, even daily; and penance, as often as we need it. The result is that we are made "holy and blameless and irreproachable before him" (Col. 1:22). This is what Christ does to us, and through our good life, we can sanctify ourselves still further. "Christ loved the church and gave himself up for her, that he might sanctify her, having cleansed her by the washing of water with the word, that he might present the church to himself in splendor, without spot or wrinkle or any such thing, that she might be holy and without blemish" (Eph. 5:25–27).

Christ's Death Gives Peace to Our Consciences

"I have said this to you, that in me you may have peace. In the world you have tribulation; but be of good cheer, I have overcome the world." (John 16:33)

Jesus Christ came into the world to give us his peace, which is not like the peace that the world gives. "Peace I leave with you," he says; "my peace I give to you; not as the world gives do I give to you" (John 14:27). His peace is something that only he can give, for only he removed God's enmity against us for our sins. In reality, it is God who always loved us, who sent us his Son to remove the enmity he had against us on account of our sins. Christ did this by satisfying divine justice through his suffering on the cross for our sins. It is this reality, and the revealed knowledge concerning it, that gives such peace to our consciences. We know, through faith, that our forgiveness is *just*, that it does not violate justice, that our just debt and just punishment have been duly paid. To know this gives peace to our consciences, the peace of Christ, which only he can give.

We have, moreover, risen with him to a new life. He sanctifies us through his justification. Christ's perfect righteousness is given to us, making us *truly* righteous and resplendent before God, and we can then grow every day more in holiness through him living within us.

No other religion can give peace to the human heart and conscience as Jesus Christ can because he alone suffered our punishment to *justly* justify us. It is this justification through his death that gives us such peace, a peace that the world cannot give. "The chastisement of our *peace* was upon him," prophesied Isaiah (Isa. 53:5 KJV). Through his suffering our punishment on the cross comes our peace. By his suffering our punishment, we were justified, made just, made righteous; and through this justification comes our peace. "Therefore being justified by faith, we have *peace* with God through our Lord Jesus Christ" (Rom. 5:1 KJV).

We have peace, then, in Jesus Christ, peace in our hearts and peace in our consciences. In the first order, Christ did not reconcile *us* with God, but rather *God* with us by satisfying God's justice and wrath through his death on the cross. God could then forgive us in all justice. It is this *just* forgiveness that gives us peace. It is a peace that comes from knowing that it was all done *justly*. This, then, is a peace that will sustain us through the tribulation we will suffer in the world. Christ therefore tells us, "Be of good cheer, I have overcome the world" (John 16:33).

Sanctified by the Law

"And the Pharisees and scribes asked him, Why do your disciples not live according to the traditions of the elders, but eat with hands defiled?"
(Mark 7:5)

We see here that Jesus and his disciples do not follow the various traditions that the Pharisees added on to the Law of Moses. We also see that as the Messiah, Jesus is superior to the Mosaic Law itself and can and does abrogate its ceremonial aspect (not its moral part—not the Ten Commandments). He abrogated the Jewish dietary laws, which were part of the Mosaic Law, when he said, "There is nothing outside a man which by going into him can defile him; but the things which come out of a man are what defile him" (Mark 7:15). And St. Mark tells us, "Thus he declared all foods clean" (Mark 7:19).

It is clear throughout the New Testament that the life, death, and resurrection of Jesus Christ justify us, not our observance of the law, whether ceremonial or moral. We do not have the power to justify ourselves before God by our own good works according to the law. It is too difficult, and no one has ever been able to do it. What does justify us is the obedient life and death of Jesus Christ. His obedience is counted as justice for us. It is imputed to us as though it were our *own* obedience. And still more, his death on the cross is the payment of the punishment from God that we owe because of our sins. His suffering is, in a similar way, imputed to us, as though *we* had suffered it. In this way, the law is fulfilled for us by Jesus Christ. He fulfills it for us both positively and negatively: positively, by his obedient life; and negatively, by his death, suffered in order to fulfill the punishment required by the law for our sins. So by believing in him, we are justified—that is, made righteous before God. And this is not through *our* observance of the law but through *his* observance of the law in his life and in his death. Thus do we uphold the law (Rom. 3:31) and its importance, and we also uphold faith in the works of Christ, who fulfilled the law for us.

When we say that we are justified by our faith, we do not mean that our faith is such a great virtue that God rewards and justifies us for having so much faith. Rather, we mean that the life, death, and resurrection of Jesus Christ justify us and fulfill the law for us. It is our faith that believes this, and in believing it receives its fruit, which is our justification. Our faith, therefore, is not a virtue rewarded by justification, but rather the channel through which we receive the free give of justification, which comes to us as a result of Christ's obedient life and vicarious death.

Neither the ceremonial nor the moral law justifies us—that is, our observance of the law does not justify us. So what meaning does the moral law have for us if it does not justify us? Jesus did not abrogate the moral law, yet at the same time, our observance of the moral law does not justify us. So what is its meaning for us? Its meaning is that it is involved in our sanctification once we have been justified by Jesus fulfilling the moral law for us in his life, death, and resurrection. Then, once we are already justified, forgiven, and made righteous and resplendent before God by our faith in Jesus Christ, we are to advance and grow still further in holiness by our observance of the moral law. As Christians, Christ has freed us from the ceremonial law—the washing of hands, pots, and jars, not eating pork, and the like—but we still have to study and follow all the details and implications of the Ten Commandments (the moral law), not for our justification but for our sanctification.

How important, then, is the moral law for a Christian! The following words are directed as much to us, the new Israel, as they were to the original Israel: "And now, O Israel, give heed to the *statutes* and the *ordinances* which I teach you, and *do* them; that you may live, and go in and take possession of the land which the Lord, the God of your fathers, gives you" (Deut. 4:1). "Blessed are those whose way is *blameless*, who walk in the *law* of the Lord! Blessed are those who keep his *testimonies*" (Ps. 119:1–2). "Thou hast commanded thy *precepts* to be kept diligently. O that my ways may be steadfast in keeping thy *statutes!*" (Ps. 119:4–5).

"But be *doers* of the word, and not hearers only, deceiving yourselves" (James 1:22).

So we must observe the moral law, but we must also walk in the Spirit. The Spirit of God is our internal preceptor, guiding us in a more personal and precise way and in greater detail, in accordance with the will of God for each one of us as individuals. We do not all have the same vocation. Some are married, others are priests or religious, others are monks or hermits. These do not all live the Ten Commandments in exactly the same way, and there are many differences in their lives and styles of living. It is the Holy Spirit, then, who will guide each one to know in detail how he should live in accordance with his own state in life. Some will need much more solitude and silence than others, and will hence not be able to do what others can do. And this is in accordance with the will of God for them. Each also has his own personal vocation, or even at times his own vocation within a vocation, and the Holy Spirit is his guide and mentor in all of this.

In summary, then, justified by faith, not by the works of the law, we are sanctified by the works of the law and guided by the Holy Spirit.

Do the Will of God

"For no good tree bears bad fruit, nor again does a bad tree bear good fruit; for each tree is known by its own fruit"
(Luke 6:43–44)

"Christ Jesus came into the world to save sinners," says St. Paul. Christ redeemed us and paid the price of our ransom in his suffering and death on the cross. Thus did he free us from the penalty of eternal death for our sins and from our guilt so that we might rise with him in his resurrection to a new and illumined life, full of the love of God, clothed in the splendor of the righteousness of Christ himself. He wants us now therefore to walk in the newness of life with the risen Christ (Rom. 6:4) and live—in the newness of the Spirit (Rom. 7:6)—a new kind of life in this world, namely one that is obedient to the will of God.

Redeemed by Jesus Christ, we should now obey God and do his will. This is why he redeemed us. We do not redeem ourselves. He alone paid the price of our redemption from eternal death by his blood poured out on the cross. And he alone justifies us, that is, only he makes us righteous, forgiven, and resplendent before God—lights in the world for others (Matt. 5:14–16; Phil. 2:15). We do not justify ourselves by our own good works or by our observance of the moral law. Once justified, though, by the death of Jesus Christ, which justification we receive through faith, then we are henceforth to *do* the will of God. Only in this way will we *remain* righteous in his sight, and only in this way will we *grow* further in holiness. We must bear good fruit. Our fruits in doing the good works of obedience will show what kind of tree we are, whether good or bad.

"Not everyone who says to me, Lord, Lord, shall enter the kingdom of heaven," says Jesus, "but he who does the will of my Father who is in heaven" (Matt. 7:21). Jesus asked, "Who is my mother, and who are my brethren?" and added, "Whoever does the will of my Father in heaven is my brother, and sister and mother" (Matt. 12:48, 50). How important it then is to do the will of God! Only those who do it will enter heaven and be close to Christ. A woman once said, "Blessed is the womb that bore you, and the breasts that you sucked! But he said, Blessed rather are those who hear the word of God and keep it!" (Luke 11:27–28). Doing God's will must be our way of life. Jesus said, "Abide in my love. If you keep my commandments, you will abide in my love, just as I have kept my Father's commandments and abide in his love" (John 15:9–10).

The will of God is that we live for him with all our hearts and love our neighbors (Mark 12:30–31). In order to love God with all our hearts and love our neighbors, we must purify our hearts. With a purified heart we can better love God and our neighbors and use our talents, time, work, and possessions to better serve both God and our neighbors. If we are not purified of the world and its pleasures, we will not love God with all our hearts. And if we do not love God with all our hearts, we will not be doing the will of God, but rather our own will. Mortification is, therefore, essential to doing the will of God. Then, instead of serving and entertaining ourselves, we will serve our neighbor with our talents, time, and possessions.

This is the purpose and result of Jesus's atoning work. It puts us into a new state before God, reconciled with him, and he with us, by the blood of Christ, which satisfies his wrath against our sins. We are, therefore, henceforth to live for he who saved us and walk in his light by doing his will.

Washed in Christ's Blood

"But when Christ had offered for all time a single sacrifice for sins, he sat down at the right hand of God … For by a single offering he has perfected for all time those who are sanctified."
(Heb. 10:12, 14)

How much we need this! We have a practically continual need for this salvation, which only Jesus Christ can give us. We have so many imperfections, and we fail in so many things to reach the degree of perfection that we wish, and that God wishes for us, that we often cry out with St. Paul, "Wretched man that I am! Who will deliver me from this body of death?" (Rom. 7:24). And our answer is the same as St. Paul's: "Thanks be to God through Jesus Christ our Lord!" (Rom. 7:25). We cry out like this because, with St. Paul, we see how many times we fail to reach perfection in our actions, and because we see how so often we do not do the perfect will of God as we wish to do it, and so we say in St. Paul's words, "I do not understand my own actions. For I do not do what I want, but I do the very thing I hate" (Rom. 7:15).

We are not to conclude from these words that St. Paul was a great sinner; rather, as other saints, he was aware of his imperfections and very sensitive about his defects and faults. And is it not the same with us? To the degree that we are growing spiritually, we become ever more aware of how we fail to reach the perfection that God wants to see in us, and so we suffer from guilt even as we grow in perfection, for we are now more sensitive than we once were, when such things did not bother us. We now, as did the saintly desert fathers, weep interiorly for sins that formerly did not disturb us. Those who are less spiritually advanced find it difficult to understand how such small things can bother us.

This is why Christ came. By his sacrifice he cleanses our consciences from this guilt, from this interior suffering. Hebrews says, "how much more shall the blood of Christ, who through the eternal Spirit offered himself without blemish to God, purify your conscience from dead works to serve the living God" (Heb. 9:14). The blood of Christ cleanses our consciences from guilt because he suffered in our place this same kind of suffering of alienation from God, of the punishment of God, of the wrath of God, the frown of God, the discipline of God (Heb. 12:5–11), being made a curse for us by being hanged on a tree (Gal. 3:13; Deut. 21:23) so we could be redeemed from all this (2 Cor. 5:21). By his suffering, we are freed from this kind of suffering, which is the worst of all suffering, for it is ourselves attacking ourselves interiorly. So we are freed by Christ's suffering, that is, until we fall into another imperfection or sin, when he will free us again and will wash us anew in his blood if we invoke him.

Jesus Christ is the one "who loves us and has freed us from our sins by his blood" (Rev. 1:5). St. Paul says, "Since, therefore, we are now justified by his blood, much more shall we be saved by him from the wrath of God" (Rom. 5:9). "The wrath of God" (Rom. 1:18) is his punishment, his discipline (Heb. 12:5–11) that shows us his will and dissuades us from offending him. St. John also tells us, "The blood of Jesus his Son cleanses us from all sin" (1 John 1:7). And St. Peter says the same: "You know that you were ransomed … with the precious blood of Christ" (1 Pet. 1:18–19).

Forgiveness for Unwitting Sins

*"But he holds his priesthood permanently, because he continues forever.
Consequently he is able for all time to save those who draw near to
God through him, since he always lives to make intercession for them."*
(Heb. 7:24–25)

We now have this great high priest, Jesus Christ, "who is seated at the
right hand of the throne of the Majesty in heaven, a minister in the
sanctuary and the true tent which is set up not by man but by the
Lord" (Heb. 8:1–2). He is now in heaven, the true sanctuary, where
he is always interceding for us with the Father (Heb. 7:25; 9:24; Rom.
8:34; 1 John 2:1). He has a better priesthood than the Levitical priesthood; a better tabernacle, heaven; a better sacrifice, himself, offered
once and for all; and a better covenant, the new covenant, prophesied
by Jeremiah (Heb. 8:8–12; Jer. 31:31–34).

This priest's sacrifice is truly effective, erasing our sins and guilt and
clothing us in his own righteousness, causing us to feel truly forgiven
when the effects of his ministry are communicated to us through his
sacrament (Matt, 18:18; John 20:23), through the hands of his earthly
representatives, the priests of his Church.

This is of great importance, for as we grow spiritually, we become
ever more sensitive about the imperfections that we fall into without
intending them. An indication of our spiritual growth is that smaller
and smaller imperfections, things that previously never bothered us,
trouble us more and more and wound our consciences. Even unwitting
and unintentional sins trouble us as we grow more in the Lord. We

discover that God not only disciplines us for known and intended sins (Heb. 12:5–11) but even for things that we fall into without intending it, and even without knowing that they are sins or imperfections. We discover that God disciplines us by giving us the pain of guilt in our hearts for these unwitting imperfections in order to teach us his will more perfectly so we will grow in perfection, and in the future avoid these actions that we now know, through his discipline, are displeasing to him. Even in the Old Testament, the Israelites were taught that God is also displeased by our unwitting sins, for he gave them various sacrifices to be offered for "unwitting sins," once these sins became known, and the people realized that they had sinned (Lev. 4:13, 22, 27).

But God then gives us relief after disciplining and punishing us for our unintentional imperfections and unwitting sins. He has sent us his only Son, Jesus Christ, as our great high priest. In him, we have a priest who offers sacrifice for the remission of our imperfections or sins, and his sacrifice is truly effective and gives us relief and great peace and happiness of spirit when its effects are channeled to us through the sacrament of reconciliation, which he established and left us for this purpose (Matt. 18:18; John 20:23).

God knows our psychological needs and how we operate. That is why he gave us this sacrament that is so psychologically effective and so satisfying, making God's forgiveness in Christ something truly experiential. Those who have not experienced this sacrament do not know the full justification and transformation that God works in us through the death of his Son on the cross. This is why the Catholic tradition has always spoken of a *real* transformation, not just a *forensic* justification. We are really justified, that is, *made* just and righteous by God. Some, who do not experience the sacrament of reconciliation, apparently do not have this complete experience of actually being *made* righteous, and so they believe say and that God only *declares* us to be just but does not really *make* us just.

The Lord Chastises and Disciplines Our Consciences

"Come unto me, all ye that labour and are heavy laden,
and I will give you rest."
(Matt. 11:28 KJV)

Christ is the great rest for our souls. With his rest and peace, we can face any problem with happiness of heart. What is it that robs us of peace? More than anything else, it is sin, or any fault that we commit, anything that we do that we know does not please God. When we do such things, we often fall into a great pit of sadness and depression, out of which we cannot extricate ourselves. Only Jesus Christ can do that for us. And it is precisely for this that he was sent into the world, to redeem us from our sins, to renew us interiorly.

This redemption is not something he only did for us at the beginning of our new lives of faith. Rather, it is something that accompanies us throughout our whole lives, all our days, for we often fall into new errors, new imperfections, which trouble us and torment our spirit, even though they are often not even venial sins, but rather simply imperfections into which we fall for lack of attention and proper reflection, or from weakness of will, or even completely inadvertently, without realizing that we are doing anything wrong at all. But even so, some of these imperfections, even inadvertent ones, can still sadden our hearts and darken our spirits, as God disciplines and flogs our consciences. He can afflict our consciences even for inadvertent imperfections, to make us aware of his will with greater precision and notify us that we are not following it perfectly. Those that are more advanced in the way of perfection are more sensitive in this matter and therefore suffer more from this. We are all, therefore, in constant need of the salvation and rest of Jesus Christ in our daily lives.

"Come unto me," Jesus says, "all ye that labour and are heavy laden, and I will give you rest" (Matt. 11:28 KJV). He is our peace. The price of our peace was upon him. His sacrifice on the cross is our *daily* remedy, the medicine of our souls, the cure of our wounds. "The chastisement of our peace was upon him; and with his strips we are healed" (Isa. 53:5 KJV).

He suffered on the cross so the wounds of our souls might be healed. We are wounded for our errors and faults, for our sins and imperfections. These wounds are God's punishments, God's discipline, to teach us, "for the Lord disciplines him whom he loves, and chastises every son whom he receives … for what son is there whom his father does not discipline?" (Heb. 12:6–7). Those who obey him more carefully are flogged the more, to perfect them still further: "For the Lord disciplines whom he loves" (Heb. 12:6). Indeed, "Those whom I love, I reprove and chasten," says the Lord (Rev. 3:19).

But then, lest we faint away and lose hope, when we look to his Son in faith and prayer, he forgives us and stops flogging our consciences, for his Son came precisely for this purpose, to be flogged and disciplined in our place, as our substitute, and to suffer abandonment by God and being cursed by God, "having become a curse for us" (Gal. 3:13), to free us from this abandonment and curse.

Look to him, and you will be saved. He will give you rest for your soul. If you persevere in prayer and petition to him, he will give you rest and will restore your soul in peace, filling you with his own righteousness, making you holy and resplendent in his sight, to live still more carefully in the future so as not to lose his great peace again.

What the prophet Isaiah said is true: "Thou dost keep him in perfect peace, whose mind is stayed on thee, because he trusts in thee" (Isa. 26:3). He is our peace, our healing, our restoration, our joy. In him is forgiveness; and by his wounds, our punishment is paid so that we might go free, justified, clothed in divine righteousness, and full of light. Let us persevere, then, in the prayer and petition of faith in Jesus Christ, until all this has been accomplished in us.

Part II:
The Vicarious Nature of Christ's Death and Its Consequences

Who Can Endure an Anguished Spirit?

"Taking her by the hand, he said to her, 'Talitha cumi'; which means, 'Little girl, I say to you, arise.' And immediately the girl got up and walked."
(Mark 5:41–42)

Jesus Christ cured many people during his life on earth, and even raised the dead, as he did to this twelve-year-old girl, to Lazarus (John 11:43), and to the son of the widow of Nain (Luke 7:14). We continue to read the gospels with faith because this same Jesus Christ, who did these things during his earthly life, is the one who is now seated in glory at the right hand of his Father in heaven, interceding with him for us (Rom. 8:34; Heb. 7:25; 9:24). As Jairus begged his help for his daughter, so do we beg his help to save us and raise us out of the death of sin.

Sin causes us more interior suffering and pain of heart than anything else. The suffering caused by our sins or imperfections, which is the suffering of guilt, is worse than all the sufferings of the body, worse than the sufferings of sickness, and worse than the suffering caused by the attacks of our enemies. This is because our own consciences are attacking us interiorly. We are attacking ourselves, and in such a situation, there is no peace, and we feel bad and unhappy.

Guilt is a sickness of the heart that no earthly medicine can cure. We can endure bodily illnesses and even the attacks and damage done to us by our enemies with a joyful spirit that comes to us from God and with inner peace and happiness. We can even endure being humiliated by our enemies and put up with it with inner happiness if we are at peace with God. But no one can endure well the suffering and pain of heart that comes from ourselves attacking ourselves for having sinned. No one can bear well the suffering in his heart caused by his own conscience continually attacking him. This is the worst suffering of all. "A man's spirit will endure sickness," says Proverbs, "but a broken spirit who can bear?" (Prov. 18:14).

It is to cure this broken spirit, this sickness of the heart, that Christ came into the world. He can raise us from the death of our spirit. For this, he died on the cross, weighed down with our sins (2 Cor. 5:21; Isa. 53:5–6) to deliver us from eternal death and the fear of it and to raise us up from the spiritual death of alienation from God and guilt. He suffered so that we would suffer no more from guilt. Our punishment of guilt was put upon him, and he suffered this alienation from God, this just wrath of God, this being cursed by God (Gal. 3:13; Deut. 21:23), this frown of God, for the sake of our sins. He suffered it for us, and instead of us, to free us from this most terrible of all suffering if only we believe in him and invoke the merits of his death for us on the cross. It is a particularly rich experience of forgiveness when we invoke the merits of his death through the sacrament that he himself left us in order to channel these merits to us personally and individually in a real and experiential way (Matt. 18:18; John 20:23).

A Remedy for the Pain of Guilt

"And when Jesus saw their faith, he said to the paralytic, My son,
your sins are forgiven' ... 'But that you may know that the Son
of Man has authority on earth to forgive sins'—he said to the
paralytic—'I say to you, rise, take up your pallet and go home.'"
(Mark 2:5, 10–11)

Everyone was astounded to hear these words of Jesus, telling the paralytic that his sins are forgiven. The scribes said, "Why does this man speak thus? It is blasphemy! Who can forgive sins but God alone?" (Mark 2:7). This was indeed something new, something extraordinary. It is an indication of Jesus's divinity, for only God can forgive sins, as the scribes correctly point out. Even though Jesus did not say he absolved him of his sins, but only "your sins are forgiven" (Mark 2:5), it is still an indication of his divinity, for who—except God alone— knows that this man's sins have been forgiven? And who—but God alone—has the authority to assure someone that his sins have been forgiven? And this is precisely the great novelty that we see here, that Jesus Christ, the Son of Man, has power on earth even to forgive sins. He also forgave the sins of the woman who washed his feet with her tears and dried them with her hair (Luke 7:48). Then, to prove that he really does have this power and that this man's sins truly have been forgiven, he cured him of his paralysis.

What could be worse than sin? We can endure even with joy any other problem or sickness, even martyrdom if the risen Christ is shining in our hearts (2 Cor. 4:6), filling us with light and the joy of the Holy Spirit, as rivers of living water, running through our interiors (John 7:37–39), rejoicing us within. But sin is different. Sin darkens and saddens the spirit, causing depression, anguish, and pain in the heart.

The saints, who are very sensitive, were in anguish even over very small imperfections. What joy, then, to hear that there is a remedy here on earth for this worst of all sicknesses, for this sickness of the soul, for this sadness and depression, for this pain of heart, for which there is no human remedy.

The good news is that, since the days of Jesus Christ, there is now a remedy on earth for the anguished spirit. There is a remedy for guilt. The Son of Man does indeed have "authority on earth to forgive sins" (Mark 2:10). And not only that, but he also gave this power to his apostles so his Church might always have this power on earth.

After his resurrection, Jesus appeared to his apostles on Easter evening and said to them, "As the Father has sent me, even so I send you. And when he had said this, he breathed on them, and said to them, Receive the Holy Spirit. If you forgive the sins of any, they are forgiven; if you retain the sins of any, they are retained" (John 20:21–23). This is the great wonder that Jesus gave to his Church—namely the same power on earth that he himself had to forgive sins and give us relief from this greatest sickness of all, from this sadness of the soul, from this depression of the spirit. And we see that he sends out his ministers to do this, just as he himself was sent out to forgive sins on earth. "As the Father has sent me," he says, "even so I send you" (John 20:21).

We especially experience this wonder, this great relief for the worst of our sufferings on earth, in the sacrament of reconciliation. In this sacrament, we receive the same relief and the same healing for our anguished spirit that this paralytic received when the Son of Man pronounced him forgiven for all his sins and relieved of all the anguish and depression of his spirit.

How often do we ask God in our hearts for forgiveness for a certain sin or imperfection that agonizes our spirits, but we still continue to be in anguish? But then, on the other hand, how often have we confessed our sin or imperfection in the sacrament of reconciliation and come out feeling completely forgiven, happy, renewed, truly justified, and at peace with God? This is the wonder of this sacrament, given to us by Christ, that there is now on earth the power to forgive us our sins and to heal this great illness of our spirit. Jesus has sent out his ministers to perform this ministry.

Only God has the power to forgive sins—as the scribes correctly noted—and Jesus Christ, the only Son of God, equal to the Father in divinity, exercised this power on earth; and after his resurrection, he gave it to his Church, to his apostles, so that this ministry would always remain in his Church for the salvation and relief of those who believe in him. Such power has God given to his elect, even the power to cure this most anguishing of all sicknesses, the depression of spirit caused by sin or by imperfections, caused by our own consciences attacking us! God has so loved us that he has given us this power! Jesus Christ promised to give this power to Peter when he said, "I will give you the keys of the kingdom of heaven, and whatever you bind on earth shall be bound in heaven, and whatever you loose on earth shall be loosed in heaven" (Matt. 16:19). Here is the power to loosen us from our sins; and as it is ministered to us on earth, so will it be accomplished for us in heaven, as Jesus promised—what is loosed on earth will be loosed in heaven. In this way, Jesus Christ wanted this power to remain on earth after his ascension to help us and give us relief for this great anguish of the human spirit. Jesus then later gave this same power to all the apostles (Matt. 18:18; John 20:23).

This is truly a new thing on earth and a great wonder!

Victory over the Fear of Death

"Therefore he had to be made like his brethren in every respect, so
that he might become a merciful and faithful high priest in the service
of God, to make propitiation for the sins of the people."
(Heb. 2:17)

Jesus Christ came into the world to propitiate God for our sins through
his death on the cross, and thus by his death free us from death and
from the devil, "who has the power of death" (Heb. 2:14). In other
words, Christ came "that through death he might destroy him who has
the power of death, that is, the devil, and deliver all those who through
fear of death were subject to lifelong bondage" (Heb. 2:15).

Death is the result of sin (Gen. 2:16–17; Rom. 6:23; 5:12; Wis. 1:13;
2:23–24), and so in expiating sin, Christ destroyed the power of death,
the power of the devil. He propitiated for and expiated sin by means of
his own death. St. John says, "If anyone does sin, we have an advocate
with the Father, Jesus Christ the righteous; and he is the propitiation
for our sins, and not for ours only but also for the sins of the whole
world" (1 John 2:12). And he also says that God "sent his Son to be the
propitiation for our sins" (1 John 4:10).

Christ propitiated and placated the wrath of God against our sins by
suffering himself this wrath and this abandonment by God on the cross,
thus absorbing and propitiating all the divine wrath against the sin of
man. This is why Jesus "began to be troubled and deeply distressed" in
Gethsemane, saying, "My soul is exceedingly sorrowful, even to death"
(Mark 14:33–34 NKJV). This was because he knew that he was going
to suffer not only death, but also the wrath of God and separation from
him—alienation from him. This is why he cried out in anguish from the
cross, "My God, my God, why hast thou forsaken me" (Matt. 27:46).

It is more than death that he suffered. He also suffered separation from God, abandonment by him, and God's wrath in suffering the just punishment for all the sins of the world. He suffered the curse of God on the cross (Gal. 3:13), when "For our sake he [God] made him to be sin who knew no sin, so that in him we might become the righteousness of God" (2 Cor. 5:21). That is, God laid upon him all our sins, to expiate them and propitiate God for them by his death, so that we might be made righteous with the righteousness of Christ himself.

Having propitiated the Father for our sins, Christ saved us from the fear of death as separation from God and punishment of eternal fire. Now, therefore, for those who believe in him, death has lost its power. "Death is swallowed up in victory. O death, where is thy victory? O death, where is thy sting? The sting of death is sin" (1 Cor. 15:54–56). With Christ's death intervening, we are freed from the fear of death. We have victory over death and over the fear of death through the death of Jesus Christ our Lord.

Jesus Conquers Spiritual Death

"He said, Depart; for the girl is not dead but sleeping. And they
laughed at him. But when the crowd had been put outside, he went
in and took her by the hand, and the girl arose."
(Matt. 9:24–25)

We see here that Jesus Christ is victorious over death. He could raise
this girl from the dead, as he raised Lazarus and the son of the widow
of Nain from the dead. Jesus has this power because he came to expiate
the sin of Adam and the sins of all his children. Because death entered
the world as the punishment for the sin of Adam (Gen. 2:17), in expiating this sin by his death on the cross, Christ also conquered death.
By raising the dead, he demonstrated that he was indeed the victor
over death; and his own resurrection was the ultimate proof that he is
the conqueror of death.

Spiritual death—that is, separation from God—is also the result of
sin, and if one does not repent, he will die eternally when he dies physically. Jesus Christ came to free us from spiritual death and to change our
physical death into a portal of eternal life rather than a portal of eternal
death. His death paid our debt of the punishment of death so that we
would not have to die eternally if we believe in him. He suffered death
instead of us, so we would not have to suffer it; therefore, our physical
death is changed. It is now the way of access into eternal life for those
who believe in him, and no longer the portal into eternal death.

A person who is spiritually dead—that is, separated from God by
sin—is someone who does not have true happiness, who does not have
the happiness of God in his heart. He lives, rather, in inner darkness,
guilt, and sadness. He has a great pain in his heart that he cannot cure,

and his conscience constantly accuses and attacks him. It is a life of death, on its way to eternal death.

But "if you confess with your lips that Jesus is Lord and believe in your heart that God raised him from the dead, you will be saved" (Rom. 10:9). Your sins will be expiated by his death on the cross, and the pain of guilt in your heart will disappear. You will be a new creation in Jesus Christ (2 Cor. 5:17), you will have the happiness of God in your heart, and you will sing a new song, the song of the redeemed of the Lord. You will indeed know that Jesus Christ is the conqueror of spiritual death and the victor over death.

Jesus Christ, the Victor over Death

"God created man for incorruption, and made him in the image
of his own eternity, but through the devil's envy death entered the
world, and those who belong to his party experience it."
(Wis. 2:23–24)

Death entered the world because of the sin of Adam, and all die because of his sin. He had immortality but lost it by sinning and therefore no longer had it to bequeath to his descendants. Death was the
punishment for the sin of Adam because he disobeyed the commandment of God, who said, "Of the tree of the knowledge of good and evil
you shall not eat, for in the day that you eat of it you shall die" (Gen.
2:17). St. Paul affirms this connection between sin and death, saying,
"The wages of sin is death" (Rom. 6:23), and "As sin came into the
world through one man and death through sin, and so death spread
to all men because all men sinned" (Rom. 5:12), and "Because of one
man's trespass, death reigned through that one man" (Rom. 5:17).

We note that even infants, who never personally sinned, die, not as
a punishment for their own personal sins, which they did not have, but
because of the sin of Adam. Death is a punishment for sin, and so infants
die because of the sin of Adam, not because of their own sins. St. Paul
says that even before the Law of Moses was given, everyone still died,
even though they did not disobey any revealed law. Even though their
sins were not as serious as Adam's, they still died because of Adam's sin.
St. Paul affirms this, noting that "Sin indeed was in the world before
the law was given, but sin is not counted where there is no law" (Rom.
5:13). In other words, their sin was not as serious as Adam's because
they lacked the law. But even so, they still died because of the serious-
ness of the sin of Adam. So St. Paul says, "Yet death reigned from Adam

to Moses, even over those whose sins were not like the transgressions of Adam" (Rom. 5:14), as is also the case with infants. The conclusion is that we die because of the sin of Adam. One single man was able to constitute all of us sinners—even when we were infants and had not yet personally done anything sinful—and was hence subjected to death. We die, therefore, because of Adam's sin.

In a similar way, all the elect—that is, all who believe in Jesus Christ—are constituted righteous, forgiven for their sins, and given eternal life by one man, Jesus Christ, for "As one man's trespass led to condemnation for all men, so one man's act of righteousness leads to acquittal and life for all men" (Rom. 5:18). And this justification happens when we believe in him, that is, before we have done any good thing to deserve it. As death passed to all through one man, Adam, so eternal life and victory over death came upon all the elect through one man, Jesus Christ. Christ is the victor over death for all who believe in him.

Christ conquers both spiritual and physical death. Spiritual death is separation from God, alienation from him. This is the death of the soul, the death of the spirit. Christ conquered spiritual death, which is our punishment for sin, by taking on this punishment for us. Since he suffered our punishment in our place and instead of us, we no longer have to suffer this punishment of spiritual death. Thus Christ frees us from spiritual death when we believe in him. The merits of the death of Christ erase the guilt of all the elect. The sin of Adam is forgiven for them, together with their own sins, and they can live in the light.

Christ is, at the same time, the victor over physical death as well, and we see this, for example, when he raises a twelve–year-old girl from the dead (Mark 5:41–42). He is our life and our resurrection. We see his supreme victory over physical death in his own resurrection from the dead on the third day. By his power, all who believe in him will rise bodily when he comes again in glory on the clouds of heaven. But even now he conquers our physical death, in that the death of a believer, born again in Jesus Christ, is not the same as the death of an unbeliever, nor is it like the death of a sinner not forgiven by Christ. For a believer, death is transformed into a passageway into eternal light in heaven with God and all his angels and saints.

Jesus Christ is, therefore, our great hope, the conqueror of death, he who forgives our sins and justifies and sanctifies us. When we die, he will take us to heaven to be with him in glory in ineffable light. And on the last day, he will raise us in our bodies, then glorified, to live with him forever in the world of the resurrection. We now live in this hope. It illuminates us in the darkness of the present life. Christ frees us from spiritual death, from the burden of our sins, and from the pain in our hearts caused by our guilt. He conquers for us, at the same time, both our spiritual and our physical deaths. He is the victor over death.

Rest for Our Souls

"Come to me, all who labor and are heavy laden, and I will give you rest. Take my yoke upon you, and learn from me; for I am gentle and lowly in heart, and you will find rest for your souls. For my yoke is easy, and my burden is light."
(Matt. 11:28–30)

In Jesus Christ, there is rest for our souls. Only in him can we find the true rest for our souls that we seek and yearn for. It is our sins and imperfections, more than anything else, that cause us to be heavy laden. Only God can relieve us from this burden. This is the burden of guilt, the burden of depression, caused by our sins and imperfections. Yet even this pain helps us, for it teaches us God's will for us with greater precision and motivates us to correct ourselves and learn new and better ways of behaving. We do not want to be depressed, so we avoid behavior that we know will depress us; and in this way, we live better lives, more in accord with God's will for us.

Christ's yoke, on the other hand, which is his will for us, or the way he wants us to live and the things he wants us to do, or not do, does not depress us. It is easy and light and rejoices the heart. We should, therefore, not only do his will—carry his yoke—but also bring to him our burden, sadness, depression, guilt, and sin so he can heal us and give true rest to our heavy-laden souls. Only in Christ will we feel this rest in the depth of our spirits after having become heavy laden by offending him with our imperfections.

Jesus Christ left to his Church the power to forgive sins through the merits of his death on the cross. Through the sacraments, the Church applies the blood of Christ to our hearts, wounded by our sins or imperfections, and heals us. Christ, through his sacrament of reconciliation (Matt. 18:18; John 20:23), gives us new life and happiness where there was formerly sadness and pain of heart, caused by guilt. This is why he died on the cross, to free us from this pain of alienation from God. He himself suffered this pain of alienation from his Father on the cross in our place to expiate our sins by suffering for us the punishment justly due. The only thing that he requires of us is our faith, a profession that we believe that he bore our sins and paid for us our debt of suffering in punishment for our sins.

This debt is not to be paid twice, that is, once by him and then again by us. It needs to be paid but once only, by him—not by us. By his wounds we are healed (Isa. 53:5). "The *chastisement* of our *peace* was upon him" (Isa. 53:5 KJV), for "the Lord hath laid on him the iniquity of us all" (Isa. 53:6 KJV). Because *he* was punished by God for our sins, we find in him rest for our souls. In the future, if we walk more exactly in his ways—which this pain taught us and motivated us to follow—we will live in peace. We will no longer be labored and heavy laden.

God's Wrath and Favor

"O Lord, the great and terrible God, who keeps covenant and
steadfast love with those who love him and keep his commandments
... To us, O Lord, belongs confusion of face, to our kings, to our
princes, and to our fathers, because we have sinned against thee."
(Dan. 9:4,8)

Daniel speaks of the blessing and the punishment of God, saying that
those who keep his commandments will be blessed, while those who
disobey him will be punished.

The same is true for the Christian, justified through his faith by the
merits of the death of Jesus Christ on the cross. Those who do the will of
God will be blessed and sanctified by him, while those who disobey him
will not experience his blessing but rather will live under his punishment
and wrath. The Hebrews in the Old Testament were in the same position
that we are, for they too were justified by their faith in the Messiah that
was to come (Rom. 4:3; Gen. 15:6), just as we are justified by our faith
in the Messiah that has already come (Rom. 3:21–22, 24, 28). But if
they, after being justified by their faith, sinned, then they lived under
the wrath of God; and it will be the same for us if we sin after being
justified by our faith in Jesus Christ. Then we too will suffer under God's
wrath against our sins until we confess them and God again forgives us
through the merits of Christ.

This righteous wrath of God is for our good; it is the discipline of
the Lord (Heb. 12:5–11). Therefore, "My son, do not regard lightly the
discipline of the Lord, nor lose courage when you are punished by him.
For the Lord disciplines him whom he loves, and chastises every son
whom he receives" (Heb. 12:5–6; Prov. 3:11–12). Thus, "Those whom

I love, I reprove and chasten" (Rev. 3:19). This discipline of the Lord is his righteous wrath against our sins for our good, because he loves us.

The Hebrews, who were justified by their faith in the Messiah that was to come (Rom. 4:3), experienced this wrath, and prayed: "Restore us again, O God of our salvation, and put away thy *indignation* toward us! Wilt thou be *angry* with us for ever? Wilt thou prolong thy *anger* to all generations?" (Ps. 85:4–5).

If we want to have peace, we must avoid the wrath of God by obeying him and keeping his commandments. If we obey him, we will have peace; but if we disobey God, we will lose his peace and be miserable and depressed, suffering under his righteous wrath, for our good. Yes, God is the Lord "who keeps covenant and steadfast love with those who love him and keep his commandments" (Dan. 9:4); but "To us, O Lord, belongs confusion of face, to our kings, to our princes, and to our fathers, because we have sinned against thee" (Dan. 9:8).

Thus "the Lord loves justice; he will not forsake his saints. The righteous shall be preserved for ever" (Ps. 37:28). "The meek shall possess the land, and delight themselves in abundant prosperity" (Ps. 37:11). Great is the peace of those who fear the Lord and walk in his ways, avoiding his wrath by not disobeying him.

Abraham Believed God, and It Was Reckoned to Him as Righteousness

"Your father Abraham rejoiced that he was to see my day;
he saw it and was glad."
(John 8:56)

This verse is very important because it helps us understand how God justifies human beings in every age—in the Old Testament as well as in the New. St. Paul teaches us that God always, and in every age, justifies man through his faith in Jesus Christ, not through his own works. This, he says, was as true for Abraham as it is for us. "For if Abraham was justified by works," says St. Paul, "he has something to boast about, but not before God. For what does the scripture say? Abraham *believed* God, and it was reckoned to him as *righteousness*" (Rom. 4:2–3; Gen. 15:6).

Jesus tells us that "Abraham rejoiced that he was to see my day; he saw it and was glad" (John 8:56). Upon seeing Jesus, Abraham believed, "and it was reckoned to him as righteousness" (Rom. 4:3; Gen. 15:6). Man does not justify himself. He does not justify himself through his own works but is only justified through his faith in Jesus Christ. We are justified through our faith in the merits of the death of Jesus Christ, who has already come, while Abraham and the saints of the Old Testament were justified through their faith in the Messiah that was still to come. Even their general faith in God was reckoned to them as righteousness through the merits of the future death of Jesus Christ on the cross. In any case, the method of justification is the same for all. All who are justified are justified through their faith, not through their works. The

Old Testament saints were just as much justified only by their faith as are those of the New Testament.

Jesus Christ always existed as a divine person, as the eternal Son of the Father. The person of Jesus Christ of Nazareth is the same eternal person who is the eternal Word and the eternal Son of the Father; and the Father always had a Son. Hence Jesus could say, "Truly, truly, I say to you, before Abraham was, I am" (John 8:58). He always was.

If we need to be justified and forgiven anew for our new sins or imperfections, we have to do what man has always had to do in every age, namely go to God and to the Savior with faith, believing that he will forgive us, justify us, and clothe us anew in the splendid robe of the righteousness of Jesus Christ himself. We of the New Testament know that God will justify us through the merits of the death of his only Son, who substituted himself for us on the cross, suffering the punishment for our sins to free us from this suffering and guilt that so debilitates us. And he will justify us through our faith, just as he did to Abraham and to the Old Testament saints. It will be the merits of Jesus's death on the cross that justify us, as well as the Old Testament saints.

No Other Name

"I am the door: if anyone enters by me, he will be saved,
and will go in and out and find pasture."
(John 10:9)

Jesus Christ is "the door of the sheep" (John 10:7). We are the sheep. If we go through this door, given to us by God, we will be saved and find pasture. For this, Jesus Christ came into the world, sent by the Father. He came so that we might have life, and have it to the full (John 10:10).

There is only one door, and all the sheep have to go through this one door if they want to find pasture and be saved. Jesus Christ is the only door given to man by which he can be saved. Only those who pass through him will be saved, for "there is salvation in no one else, for there is no other name under heaven given among men by which we must be saved" (Acts 4:12). This is why Peter was sent to preach Christ to Cornelius. An angel was sent to Cornelius, telling him that Peter "will declare to you a message by which you will be saved, you and all your household" (Acts 11:14). When Peter preached Christ to them, the Holy Spirit fell upon them, and Peter was surprised to see that "to the Gentiles also God has granted repentance unto life" (Acts 11:18).

This was a new discovery for the people in the early Church, who in the beginning were all Jews. They saw that when they preached Christ to the Gentiles, they too received the Holy Spirit and spoke in tongues (Acts 10:46), just as they themselves did. They realized then that they were to preach Christ to the Gentiles too, so that they too might be saved and have their sins forgiven, invoking his name. Peter preached to Cornelius's friends, saying, "To him all the prophets bear witness that everyone who believes in him receives forgiveness of sins through his name" (Acts 10:43).

Christ came into the world so this good news might be preached to "every creature" (Mark 16:15), so that everyone—not just Jews—might have the opportunity to have his sins forgiven by invoking this name with faith, and thus be saved and assured of eternal life.

There is no difference between Jews and Gentiles as far as justification and salvation are concerned. All, by nature, are under the wrath of God and the curse of the law for the sin of Adam and for their own sins. Only Jesus Christ perfectly fulfilled the law, and he suffered its curse for not keeping it, and he did so for the sake of all the elect. All who believe in him are his elect and will be forgiven for their faith (Acts 10:43). The law demanded eternal death as the punishment for sin, and Christ died for all his elect, thus fulfilling for them this requirement of the law. Thus, when a Gentile believes in him, the death of Christ pays the debt of sin and death for this Gentile. Therefore, Jesus Christ is the Savior of the Gentiles as well as of the Jews, and so is to be preached to "every creature" (Mark 16:15). We are to give to all this opportunity of having life to the full (John 10:10). The missionary vocation is to preach God's salvation in Jesus Christ to the ends of the earth. This is a salvation for all peoples of all religions. We may preach it by word of mouth or by the written word. We may preach it in print or electronically. This is a message that brings new life to all. Those who accept this preaching are the elect, predestined to eternal life. We are to make known this one door of salvation to the ends of the earth. This is the mission of the Church.

The Eucharistic Sacrifice

"For if the sprinkling of defiled persons with the blood of goats and bulls and with the ashes of a heifer sanctifies for the purification of the flesh, how much more shall the blood of Christ, who through the eternal spirit offered himself without blemish to God, purify your conscience from dead works to serve the living God."
(Heb. 9:13–14)

Christ's body and blood are the sacrifice offered to God on the cross, on Calvary, for our redemption. This one and only sacrifice of Calvary is made present for us each time that the eucharistic sacrifice is offered. The bread during the Eucharist becomes the body of Christ, and the wine becomes his blood. It is not just a symbol of his body and blood, but his true body and true blood. This is why the Eucharist is a true sacrifice, the very sacrifice of Jesus Christ, offering himself to his Father on the cross on Calvary. The Eucharist makes present for us the one and only sacrifice of Christ, offering himself to the Father on the cross. It is not a repetition of Christ's one and only sacrifice, but rather it makes us present on Calvary at the moment of his one and only sacrifice on the cross for our salvation.

So did Jesus want it to be. He wanted us to have this sacrament in order to enter into his one and only sacrifice for our salvation. We can, in fact, as his mystical body, even offer ourselves together with Christ to the Father in love and self-gift in the eucharistic sacrifice. During the celebration of the Eucharist, we make ourselves a sacrifice to the Father, together with Jesus Christ. We offer Christ to the Father, and at the same time, we offer ourselves to the Father together with him, uniting our sacrifice of ourselves with his one and only acceptable sacrifice to the Father. The Eucharist is thus our sacrifice, the perfect worship and sacrifice of the New Testament, our perfect cult and adoration of the Father. This is the only sacrifice that we have left to us today, the one sacrifice of Christ that has fulfilled all the other sacrifices of the Old Testament.

By his sacrifice of himself, Christ gave perfect worship to his Father, and infinitely pleased him for our salvation. In his death, he satisfied all the demands of divine justice, paying with his blood, poured out for us, our debt of sin in accordance with the law. He fulfilled the law for us who have not kept it, and he suffered for us the penalty prescribed by the law for those who do not keep it. His sacrifice, therefore, gives us relief from our guilt and renews us, making us new men, resplendent before God with the very splendor of Christ himself. By his sacrifice, he removed our condemnation and restored our life.

The Atoning Sacrifice of Christ

"We have been sanctified through the offering of
the body of Jesus Christ once for all."
(Heb. 10:10)

At the annunciation of the Lord, the eternal Word, the only Son of the Father, begotten and born before all time, from all eternity, became flesh in the womb of the Virgin Mary to save us from our sins.

Christ was sent into the world by the Father to suffer and die in order that God might forgive us our sins, assuming himself their just penalty so that we would not have to suffer it. Thus did God free us from our guilt, giving us a new life and clothing us with the righteousness of Jesus Christ himself so that we might be resplendent before God, made new, a new creation, born again in Jesus Christ. And Christ promised us that if we believe in him, we would live forever with him (John 6:54).

The incarnation of Jesus Christ is the incarnation of God. It is God, therefore, who, in the person of the Son, suffers on the cross our punishment due to us for our sins. This is why the Son became man—so that, possessing a human nature, he could suffer, thus satisfying the divine wrath for human sins. But being also God, his suffering had infinite value and satisfied God. ,

In the death of Jesus Christ on the cross, God satisfied his own wrath against our sins because our debt of punishment was paid by the Son. Christ suffered the wrath of God for our sins, and satisfied it, thus freeing us from this wrath and leaving us justified and transformed, made new, and sanctified. "We have been sanctified through the offering of the body of Jesus Christ once for all" (Heb. 10:10). Therefore, "by a single offering he has perfected for all time those who are sanctified" (Heb. 10:14).

In the sacrifice of Jesus Christ on the cross, we have new life. The sins, which God formerly, in his patience, passed over, are now definitively expiated (Rom. 3:25). This sacrifice is, therefore, the fountain to which we go for forgiveness and relief from our guilt when we sin or fall into an imperfection. The cross is, therefore, a fountain of happiness and spiritual liberty. With jubilation, we draw from it the waters of salvation (Isa. 12:3).

Being made new by the death of Jesus Christ on the cross, we offer the sacrifice of ourselves to the Father with him in his sacrifice on the cross. We do this in the Eucharist, offering ourselves to the Father with Jesus Christ in his great offering of himself in love to the Father on the cross. Jesus's sacrifice on the cross was his own perfect donation of himself to the Father in love, the perfect act of worship and the perfect sacrifice of adoration. We make it our own sacrifice of self-gift in love to the Father as well, offering ourselves with the Son, to the Father, in the Holy Spirit.

We do this in the eucharistic sacrifice, which is the one and only sacrifice of Calvary, made present for us. It is our atonement and our perfect act of worship. It is the one sacrifice of the New Testament by which we are saved and worship the Father, through the Son, in the Holy Spirit.

Having completed his sacrifice for our salvation, God raised Jesus Christ from the dead, showing that he accepted his sacrifice and that our sins are now definitively expiated and propitiated, and that he, in his sacrifice, is the victor over death and the giver of life. In his resurrection, we are victorious over death and walk illuminated by the light that streams from his resurrection. We rise in him to a new life. If we do his will, we remain in this light (John 8:12).

Jesus's Sacrifice, Our Only Access to the Father

"I am the way, and the truth, and the life;
no one comes to the Father, but by me."
(John 14:6)

Jesus Christ is the agent sent by the Father into the world so that all might come to the Father through him. He is the only Son of God, made man to reveal the Father to us. He alone has been in heaven with the Father and has come down from there to teach us about God.

But Jesus did much more than this. He is also the means whereby we come to the Father. "No one comes to the Father, but by me," he says (John 14:6). He is the way that brings us to the Father, for to come to the Father we must first be justified. This means that we must first be righteous and holy by perfectly fulfilling the law, without sin, so that we shine with the righteousness of God himself.

But St. Paul teaches us that, beginning with Adam, no one has ever been able to do this. He tells us that by means of the law "None is righteous, no, not one" (Rom. 3:10), and "no human being will be justified in his sight by works of the law" (Rom. 3:20). This is because no one has ever been able to perfectly keep the law. Therefore, Jesus Christ is the only way given to men by which they may come to the Father (Acts 4:12), and so "no one," he says, "comes to the Father, but by me" (John 14:6).

God himself justifies us through the death of Jesus Christ on the cross when we believe in the Son and the power of his sacrifice. Christ is our new covenant head, or representative, and he lived righteously, fulfilling all the precepts of the law for us so that his righteousness might be ours. And since the law demands the eternal death of the sinner as punishment for its violation, Jesus Christ, our representative, also fulfilled this requirement of the law for us in his death on the cross, which has infinite value since he is the only Son of God, equal in divinity with the Father. In believing in him, then, we are reconciled with God, our sins are justly expiated by his death, and we are clothed over with his own resplendent righteousness (2 Cor. 5:21; Isa. 61:10).

The Jews before Jesus Christ were also justified by him through their faith, as was Abraham (Gen. 15:6; Rom. 4:3). All who are justified and come to the Father are justified only by the death of Jesus Christ on the cross, through their faith in him. He is the way; and no one comes to the Father, but by him.

The Father Gave His Own Beloved Son for Us

"And a cloud overshadowed them, and a voice came out of the cloud,
'This is my beloved Son; listen to him.'"
(Mark 9:7)

Here, the voice of the Father, coming out of the cloud on the mount of Transfiguration, identifies Jesus as his "beloved Son" (Mark 9:7). Jesus was transfigured before Peter, James, and John; and Moses and Elijah appeared to them, speaking with Jesus (Mark 9:4). St. Luke says, "And behold, two men talked with him, Moses and Elijah, who appeared in glory and spoke of his departure (*exodon*), which he was to accomplish at Jerusalem" (Luke 9:30–31). So we see here that Jesus is the beloved Son of the Father, who is about to suffer death—"his departure" (Luke 9:31). The Father "did not spare his own Son but gave him up for us all" (Rom. 8:32), as St. Paul tells us. Abraham's sacrifice of his only beloved son, Isaac, is a type of this. God did in actuality what he commanded Abraham to do. He offered up for us his own beloved Son.

How are we to understand this mystery? So much did the Father love us that he "did not spare his own Son but gave him up for us all." (Rom. 8:32). "God so loved the world that he gave his only Son, that whoever believes in him should not perish but have eternal life" (John 3:16).

We are to live and draw life from the Son, whom the Father gave up to death on the cross for us. "In this the love of God was made manifest among us, that God sent his only Son into the world so that we might live *through* him" (1 John 4:9). We draw life from him. "And from his fullness we have all received, grace upon grace" (John 1:16). "Yet a little while," Jesus said, "and the world will see me no more, but you will see me; because I live, you will live also" (John 14:19). The very life of Jesus now, after his death and resurrection, is the source of our new life in him. He now lives in glory, and from him we draw life. He said, "As the living

Father sent me, and I live because of the Father, so he who eats me will live because of me" (John 6:57). As Jesus draws life from his Father, so we draw life from Jesus Christ glorified. It is he who shines in our hearts (2 Cor. 4:6), vivifying and illumining us, forgiving us and clothing us in his own righteousness, as in a splendid robe (Isa. 61:10).

Through our faith in the death of the only beloved Son of God on the cross, we are saved and justified, that is, made just and righteous, made a new creation, and born again for a new life in the risen Christ. We are even raised up with him now to live a new and risen life in him on this earth, henceforth seeking him and the things that are above, and no longer the things that are below (Col. 3:1–2).

Thus we live because he lives (John 14:19), and we live through him, as he lives through the Father (John 6:57). It is he who shines within us, illuminating us (2 Cor. 4:6). We contemplate Christ now in his glory as the transfigured one, for that is how he now is; and through our contemplation of him in glory, we are transformed more and more into his image through the working of the Holy Spirit (2 Cor. 3:18).

Saved by His Death and Illumined by His Resurrection

"Jesus said to them again, Peace be with you. As the Father has sent me, even so I send you. And when he had said this, he breathed on them, and said to them, Receive the Holy Spirit. If you forgive the sins of any, they are forgiven; if you retain the sins of any, they are retained."
(John 20:21–23)

Jesus Christ, the only Son of God, came into the world to save us from sin and give us a new and risen life in him. He did this because, since the sin of Adam, we have been alienated from God because of his sin, together with our own sins. We have experienced his wrath against our sins (Rom. 1:18) and suffered guilt. God wanted to forgive us, yet being just by nature, he nonetheless had to punish our sin.

It is true that he forgave the saints of the Old Testament through their sacrifices for sin, which he himself gave and taught them in his law. Yet it was not that their sins were forgiven by the power of these animal sacrifices, but rather that God forgave them through these sacrifices because they were types of the one, adequate sacrifice of his own Son, which he was to offer in the future on the cross. In other words, God, in his forbearance and patience, forgave the Old Testament saints, overlooking their sins with an eye to their definitive expiation and propitiation in the future, when his own Son would die in sacrifice on the cross for our sins (Rom. 3:25–26).

When at last the only Son of God became man, he offered himself in sacrifice on the cross, and the Father laid on him the sins of all mankind (Isa. 53:5–6; 2 Cor. 5:21), accepting his sacrifice as payment in full of the just punishment due for all our sins. This is God's plan for our salvation.

In this way, God could save us from his own righteous wrath against our sins, suffering himself their punishment on the cross in the person of his Son, and thus remain faithful to his nature as a just God.

Already dead on the cross, on the third day, the Son of God, made man, rose from among the dead and entered into the glory of God, the first fruits of the resurrection of the dead on the last day. In his resurrection into the glory of the last day, we see that his great sacrifice of himself for the forgiveness of our sins was accepted by the Father. We who believe in him and receive baptism, invoking the merits of his death for us on the cross, are saved from our sins and from the pain of guilt to rise now with him to live a new life in his light. His resurrection has become our illumination. Redeemed through our faith in him by his blood poured out for us on the cross in propitiation for our sins, we are now illumined by the splendor of his resurrection. He now shines in our hearts (2 Cor. 4:6), illuminating us from within by a light not of this world.

Thus will we rise with Christ to a new and transformed life to be a new creation, new creatures, new men. But if we fall into an imperfection or sin and again experience the wrath (Rom. 1:18) and discipline (Heb. 12:5–11) of God, we will need to repent once again, and again invoke the merits of Christ's death on the cross; and we do this especially in the sacrament that Christ has left us for this purpose, the sacrament of reconciliation (Matt. 18:18; John 20:23). Christ gave to his apostles and their successors the power to forgive our sins when he said, "Receive the Holy Spirit. If you forgive the sins of any, they are forgiven" (John 20:23). Through this sacrament of reconciliation, we can know and feel without any doubt whatsoever that we have been forgiven. This sacrament is one of the most important gifts that Christ left to his Church, by which we might be saved from our sins and guilt and rise with him to a new and illumined life.

He Rose Victorious over Death

"Then they said to him, 'What must we do, to be doing the works of God?' Jesus answered them, 'This is the work of God, that you believe in him whom he has sent.'"
(John 6:28–29)

Jesus's hearers want to know what work they should now do since he just told them, "Do not labor for the food which perishes, but for the food which endures to eternal life" (John 6:27). They want to know what labor they should therefore now do to work for the food which endures forever; and he tells them that they are to believe in the one whom God has sent. And what are they to believe about him? They will not understand clearly what they are to believe about him until he is risen from the dead and sends the Holy Spirit upon them to enlighten their understanding.

We, along with the early Christians, are the ones who can finally understand what we are to believe about him. We are to believe that Jesus Christ is the only Son of God, and that he came into the world principally to die on the cross in punishment for all the sins of all time.

Death is the punishment for sin (Gen. 2:17). God told Adam, "Of the tree of the knowledge of good and evil you shall not eat, for in the day that you eat of it you shall die" (Gen. 2:17). So now, on the cross, Jesus suffered this punishment of death, being crucified and punished as a criminal. Yet he himself had no personal sin whatsoever, but rather all our sins were charged to him, and he, being the only Son of God, bore the punishment for us, instead of us, in order to free us from this punishment of death, of eternal fire, and of guilt. Having endured this suffering, he destroyed this punishment for all those who believe in him. Eternal death in hell was no longer needed for the elect. They would no longer need to suffer it, since he suffered it for them. Death itself was therefore destroyed for the elect in his death. Christ's death is, therefore, the death of death.

Having destroyed death, he therefore rose triumphant over death. His resurrection shows his victory over death. He is now eternally victorious over death for all who believe in him. For those, therefore, who are in Christ, death is vanquished and changed. It is no longer the door leading to eternal damnation, but rather the passageway leading to eternal life with God.

How important it then is to be in Christ by believing in him. Through our faith in him, we are freed from death as a punishment, and we rise with him to a new life. We now live in the risen Christ and are, in him, victorious over death. This punishment has ended for us. In his death, he freed us from the wrath of God and from God's punishment for our sins. We, therefore, are victorious in his victory. Through his victory—which is his resurrection—we walk in the "newness of life" (Rom. 6:4).

Jesus Christ, Our Intercessor with the Father

"But Moses besought the Lord his God, and said, O Lord, why does thy wrath burn hot against thy people, whom thou hast brought forth out of the land of Egypt with great power and with a mighty hand... Turn from thy fierce wrath, and repent of this evil against thy people... And the Lord repented of the evil which he thought to do to his people."
(Ex. 32:11, 12, 14)

Here we see the wrath of God against Israel for having made and adored the golden calf. But Moses interceded with God on their behalf, and the Lord "repented of the evil which he thought to do to his people" (Ex. 32:14).

Christ fulfills this role of intercessor for us. St. Paul tells us, "Who is to condemn? Is it Christ Jesus, who died, yes, who was raised from the dead, who is at the right hand of God, who indeed *intercedes* for us?" (Rom. 8:34).

God heard the intercession of Moses. How much more will he hear the intercession of his own Son, Jesus Christ, who always intercedes for us at the right hand of the Father (Rom. 8:34; Heb. 7:25; 9:24)! Christ is our intercessor with the Father for the forgiveness of our sins. The Father himself sent him into the world for this purpose (Rom. 8:32). Being man, he can intercede on behalf of his fellow men; but being God, his intercession has infinite value.

Christ, in addition to interceding with words, as did Moses, made himself a victim to absorb the just wrath of God against our sins. And we see, furthermore, that God is not inflicting our penalty on his Son as on a being distinct from himself, but rather is inflicting it on his Son, with whom he is but one single being, one single God, possessing the same divine mind and the same divine will as himself. In other words, God is inflicting this punishment on himself, in the person of his Son, whom he sent into the world to absorb and satisfy his own just and necessary wrath against our sins out of love for us to save us from his wrath.

Hence when we fall into an imperfection or sin, and feel guilty, with our consciences accusing and attacking us, causing us sadness and pain in our hearts, we should go with faith to the intercessor provided for us by the Father himself (Rom. 8:32), and through his intercession, we will find relief from the pain of our guilt, especially when we confess our sins and receive sacramental absolution in the sacrament of reconciliation (Matt. 18:18; John 20:23), which applies the merits of Christ's death to us in a personal and individual way so that we experience it all the more effectively and deeply.

Thus does God cure our worst sickness—guilt—and give us freedom of spirit, the glorious freedom of the sons of God (Rom. 8:21). Hence Christ is our intercessor with the Father. Christ "is able for all time to save those who draw near to God through him, since he always lives to make intercession for them" (Heb. 7:25).

Christ's Priesthood

"For this Melchizedek, king of Salem, priest of the
Most High God, met Abraham… and to him Abraham
apportioned a tenth part of everything."
(Heb. 7:1–2)

The letter to the Hebrews tells us that the priesthood of Melchizedek prefigured the priesthood of Jesus Christ in that it was not Levitical and in that it was superior to the Levitical priesthood. It was superior because Abraham, the ancestor of Levi, gave tithes to Melchizedek and was blessed by Melchizedek, and "It is beyond dispute that the inferior is blessed by the superior" (Heb. 7:7), and that the inferior gives tithes to the superior. The psalmist furthermore prophesies that the Messiah would not be a priest of the Levitical line, but "according to the order of Melchizedek" (Ps. 110:4; Heb. 7:17).

Jesus Christ is an eternal priest, not like the Levitical priests that died. As a priest, his duty is to offer sacrifice, and he offers but one sacrifice for all time, the sacrifice of himself on the cross, to justify and sanctify us, "For by a single offering he has perfected for all time those who are sanctified" (Heb. 10:14).

As a priest, Christ *intercedes* for us with the Father. St. Paul tells us that it is Jesus Christ, "who is at the right hand of God, who indeed *intercedes* for us" (Rom. 8:34). And St. John says, "My little children, I am writing this to you so that you may not sin; but if anyone does sin, we have an *advocate* with the Father, Jesus Christ the righteous" (1 John 2:1). And Hebrews says that Jesus Christ "is able for all time to save those who draw near to God through him, since he always lives to make *intercession* for them" (Heb. 7:25). Hebrews also says that "Christ has entered, not into a sanctuary made with hands, a copy of the true one, but into heaven itself, now to appear in the presence of God *on our behalf* (Heb. 9:24). Christ, therefore, is our *intercessor* with the Father.

Christ intercedes for us with the Father by his once-and-for-all sacrifice of himself on the cross, whereby taking our sins upon himself (2 Cor. 5:21; Isa. 53:6), he propitiates and placates the righteous, holy, and necessary wrath of God for our sins by himself suffering their just penalty as a substitute for us (Gal. 3:13). Hence it is God himself, in his great mercy, in the person of his Son, who pays the penalty for our sins; and so both the divine justice and the divine mercy are maintained and manifested in Christ's sacrifice (Rom. 3:26).

So we see the superiority of Christ's priesthood, compared to that of Levi. Rightly did the psalmist prophesy that the Messiah would have a new kind of priesthood and would be an eternal priest when he said, "Thou art a priest forever, after the order of Melchizedek" (Ps. 110:4; Heb. 7:17). Because of his once-and-for-all sacrifice of himself, he ever makes intercession for us with the Father (Rom. 8:34; 1 John 2:1; Heb. 7:25; 9:24).

Access into the Heavenly Sanctuary

"Therefore, brethren, since we have confidence to enter the sanctuary by the blood of Jesus, by the new and living way which he opened for us through the curtain, that is, through his flesh, and since we have a great priest over the house of God, let us draw near with a true heart in full assurance of faith, with our hearts sprinkled clean from an evil conscience and our bodies washed with pure water."
(Heb. 10:19–22)

This is what we now have in Jesus Christ: new access into the heavenly sanctuary through the flesh of Christ, which is like a veil through which we now pass and thus enter into this sanctuary, to be in the presence of God. We have this new access through the blood of Jesus Christ, poured out in sacrifice for us, to wash our consciences and our hearts that they might be purified from sin and from every spot. And so it is, for a death has intervened for the remission of our sins (Heb. 9:15). His death frees us from the death of separation from God in that he suffered for us our punishment for our sins so that we might go free now from this punishment of guilt, having this new access to the Father, not just once a year, and not just for the high priest entering into the earthly sanctuary, but all the time, and for every believer.

This is the Christian life, the new life we now have in Christ through our faith. Through him, we can live with our hearts freed from the pain of guilt and rejoice in the Holy Spirit. We should, therefore, now approach God through Jesus Christ "in full assurance of faith, with hearts sprinkled clean from an evil conscience" (Heb. 10:22). "Let us then with confidence draw near to the throne of grace" (Heb. 4:16), for, as Jesus says, "I am the way, the truth, and the life; [and] no one comes to the

Father but by me" (John 14:6). He is the veil of access through whom we must now pass. We eat his flesh, and so enter by means of him into the presence of God; and his sacrificed blood cleanses us, absorbing the divine wrath against our sins. It is "through him" that we "have access in one Spirit to the Father" (Eph. 2:18). In him, "we have boldness and confidence of access through our faith in him" (Eph. 3:12). At the death of Jesus, "the curtain of the temple was torn in two, from top to bottom" (Mark 15:38), indicating that access to God is now available through the intervening death of the Son of God.

Truly "shall the blood of Christ, who through the eternal Spirit offered himself without blemish to God, purify your conscience from dead works to serve the living God" (Heb. 9:14). This is because "In him we have redemption through his blood, the forgiveness of our trespasses" (Eph. 1:7). He comes to us through faith and through his sacraments to cleanse our hearts and our consciences through the merits of his death on the cross so that we might be alive to God.

This makes all the difference in the world for us personally and experientially. It is the difference between being depressed and filled with the pain of guilt on the one hand, and being liberated and cleansed by God's justice on the other hand, for our penalty has been paid for us, and we are acquitted and set free to rejoice in the freedom of the sons of God (Rom. 8:21). It is the difference between depression because of guilt, and jubilation of spirit for being redeemed by the blood of Jesus Christ, shed in sacrifice and propitiation of the Father's wrath for us on the cross, making us clean and new, and filled with joy in the Holy Spirit. This is something real and experiential. It is the difference between life and death. It marks for us the beginning of a new life in God through faith in his Son, Jesus Christ.

The Lamb of God Who Takes Away the Sins of the World

"The next day again John was standing with two of his disciples;
and he looked at Jesus as he walked, and said,
Behold, the Lamb of God!"
(John 1:35)

The previous day, John the Baptist had said, "Behold, the Lamb of God, who takes away the sin of the world" (John 1:29). For this reason, Jesus Christ came into the world, to take away our sins so that we might be free from the sadness that is the depression and pain in the heart caused by guilt, so that we might walk free in the glorious freedom of the children of God (Rom. 8:21). The guilt that depresses us comes from the just wrath of God against our sins (Rom. 1:18).

God is, at the same time, both just and loving. In his justice, he hates and punishes all sin. We see the wrath of God everywhere in the Bible. It is right in Eden. God said to Adam in Eden that on the day he eats from the forbidden tree of the knowledge of good and evil, he will die (Gen. 2:17), that is, experience God's wrath for his sin of disobedience, and become mortal. Death, separation from God, and alienation from him was the punishment for original sin. We see the wrath of God in the flood, in the days of Noah, when God destroyed everything because of human wickedness. We see it again in the destruction of Sodom and Gomorrah. The Psalms speak of the wrath of God: "Put away thy *indignation* toward us! Wilt thou be *angry* with us forever? Wilt thou prolong thy *anger* to all generations?" (Ps. 85:4–5). Jesus speaks of the rich man who feasted sumptuously every day, who was now in hell (Luke 16:19–31); he speaks of the final judgment of those who would go into eternal fire (Matt. 25:41, 46); and of the Son of Man, who would come in his glory "and then repay each one according to his works" (Matt. 16:27). St. Paul also speaks of "the wrath of God … against all ungodliness and wickedness" (Rom. 1:18). Therefore, when we sin, we feel this wrath of God burning our hearts and our consciences.

But Jesus Christ is the redeemer, whom God sent to us without sparing him ("He did not spare his own Son," Rom. 8:32), to redeem and save us from his own righteous, necessary, and holy wrath. God's wrath is not like ours, a state of being out of control; but rather is an attribute of the just God, who hates all evil and sin, and who punishes all sin in his perfect justice. Christ was, therefore, sent from God to redeem us from this wrath by suffering it himself on the cross for us so that God could remain just. In the death of Christ on the cross, the righteous and just wrath of God spent itself completely, exhausted itself on his body, dying on the cross, for Christ suffered this divine wrath in our place, being made a curse for us in being hung from a tree (Gal. 3:13).

St. Paul says that God passed over, in his patience, the sins committed in the Old Testament without punishing them adequately, and hence he seemed to be a loving and merciful God, but not a just one. But he did this, according to St. Paul, because he had his eye on the future definitive expiation of Jesus Christ on the cross, whereby he would pay the just debt and suffer the just penalty for all sin, both past and future. St. Paul says that God "put forward" Jesus Christ "as a propitiation by his blood, to be received by faith. This was to show God's justice, because in his divine forbearance he had passed over former sins" (Rom. 3:25). In other words, the death of Christ on the cross publically shows the justice of God—that is, that God is himself just, in that he does indeed justly punish all sin. God did this, says St. Paul, "to prove at the present time that he himself is just" (Rom. 3:26).

So we see in the cross that not only is God loving, but that he is also perfectly just, demanding a just punishment for all sin. In Christ's death, God's justice is maintained, shown, proven, and satisfied, in that God counts Christ's death on the cross as just punishment for all sin. But at the same time, and by the very same act of Jesus Christ, his only Son, on the cross, God also shows that he is supremely loving and merciful because he accepts the death of his own Son as adequate and sufficient punishment for all the sins of the world, for those past as well as future. All sins have been adequately and justly punished in the death of his Son on the cross.

The result is that we are definitively and justly forgiven if we believe in Christ and invoke his merits, particularly in the sacrament of reconciliation (Matt. 18:18; John 20:23). Thus this death of the Lamb of God in sacrifice does two things simultaneously, as St. Paul says. It manifests that God "himself is just, and that he justifies him who has faith in Jesus" (Rom. 3:26). Christ was "put to death for our trespasses and raised for our justification" (Rom. 4:25).

Christ therefore is the lamb of sacrifice, "who gave himself as a ransom for all" (1 Tim. 2:6). Hence God himself, in his love for us, saves us from his own righteous wrath against our sins by suffering himself, in the person of his Son, our punishment so that we might go free from punishment and from the suffering of guilt. Christ, therefore, was for us "like a lamb that is led to the slaughter" (Isa. 53:7). "But he was wounded for our transgressions, he was bruised for our iniquities; upon him was the chastisement that made us whole, and with his stripes we are healed… and the Lord laid on him the iniquity of us all" (Isa. 53:5–6).

We are now, therefore, new men, living in the light of his resurrection, made righteous with the righteousness of Jesus Christ himself, "For Christ, our paschal lamb, has been sacrificed" (1 Cor. 5:7).

He Will Bring Forth Righteousness

"And when he came up out of the water, immediately he saw
the heavens opened and the Spirit descending upon him like
a dove; and a voice came from heaven, Thou art my beloved
Son; with thee I am well pleased."
(Mark 1:10–11)

This is the baptism of the Lord, and the voice of his Father identifies
him as his beloved Son and his servant in whom he is well pleased (Isa.
42:1). He is thus the fulfillment of the prophecies of Isaiah about the
suffering servant of the Lord who would redeem his people from their
sins (Isa. 53). Jesus is, therefore, the one who is anointed by the Holy
Spirit to "bring forth righteousness to the nations" (Isa. 42:1). "He will
faithfully bring forth righteousness. He will not fail or be discouraged
till he has established righteousness in the earth" (Isa. 42:3–4). He will
be given as "a light to the nations" (Isa. 42:6). He will come "to open
the eyes that are blind, to bring out the prisoners from the dungeon,
from the prison those who sit in darkness" (Isa. 42:7). Jesus is the one
sent to bring us joy and light.

Jesus acknowledged himself to be this servant when the messengers
of John the Baptist asked him, "Are you he who is to come, or shall we
look for another? And Jesus answered them, Go and tell John what you
hear and see: the blind receive their sight and the lame walk, lepers are
cleansed and the deaf hear, and the dead are raised up, and the poor
have the good news preached to them" (Matt. 11:3–5).

Jesus again acknowledges himself to be this servant, anointed by the
Spirit to free his people, when in the synagogue in Nazareth he said,
"Today this scripture has been fulfilled in your hearing" (Luke 4:21).
And the scripture was, "The Spirit of the Lord is upon me, because he

has anointed me to preach good news to the poor. He has sent me to proclaim release to the captives and recovering of sight to the blind, to set at liberty those who are oppressed" (Luke 4:18; Isa. 61:1).

And now at his baptism we see this servant of the Lord, this beloved Son of God, upon whom the Holy Spirit descended "like a dove" (Mark 1:11). He brings righteousness to the earth. He justifies those who believe in him. Through the offering of himself on the cross, he frees us from our sins and clothes us in glory, as in a splendid robe of righteousness (Isa. 61:10). He came to free us from the burden of our sin and guilt, that we might live in the freedom and happiness of the children of God (Rom. 8:21). He is our light, for he has been given as "a light to the nations" (Isa. 42:6) to bring us out of the dungeon of our alienation from God.

On the cross, Christ suffered in our place and for our sake the suffering that we would have had to undergo for our sins, had he not suffered it for us. He suffered our penalty for us in order that we would not have to suffer it again, and so could thus be freed from the punishment of guilt and eternal death. He is, therefore, our light and our happiness, freeing us from the darkness of sin, guilt, and death.

Jesus Christ is the suffering servant of the Lord, who "carried our sorrows" (Isa. 53:4) on the cross. In God's justice, it was necessary that sinners suffer a just penalty for their sins. And God so loved us that he sent his own Son to suffer this punishment for us in order to free us from it and thereby be able to *justly* forgive our sins (Rom. 8:32).

Jesus is the suffering servant prophesied by Isaiah who "has borne our griefs" (Isa. 53:4); and "the Lord has laid on him the iniquity of us all" (Isa. 53:6). "He was cut off from the land of the living, stricken for the transgression of my people" (Isa. 53:8). "He makes himself an offering for sin" (Isa. 53:10). "He shall bear their iniquities" (Isa. 53:11). "He poured out his soul to death … yet he bore the sin of many" (Isa. 53:12). "But he was wounded for our transgressions, he was bruised for our iniquities; upon him was the chastisement that made us whole, and with his stripes we are healed" (Isa. 53:5).

In Jesus Christ, we have the forgiveness of our sins when we invoke in faith the merits of his death on the cross. "To him all the prophets bear witness," said St. Peter, "that everyone who believes in him receives forgiveness of sins through his name" (Acts 10:43). And Peter and John also said, "God exalted him at his right hand as Leader and Savior, to give repentance to Israel and forgiveness of sins" (Acts 5:31).

What better news is there than this—that in Jesus Christ, through faith in him, our sins are definitively expiated and forgiven, and that we are now free from the heavy, painful, and depressing burden of guilt and the prospects of eternal death. We are set free from this punishment to enjoy the freedom of the children of God (Rom. 8:21). Christ has freed us. He has clothed us in his own righteousness, as in a splendid robe (Isa. 61:10); and we have clothed ourselves in Jesus Christ (Gal. 3:27; Rom. 13:14).

"For our sake he made him to be sin who knew no sin, so that in him we might become the righteousness of God" (2 Cor. 5:21). In other words, God made Jesus Christ "to be sin" by laying upon him our sins in order to expiate them through his death on the cross so that we might be clothed in his righteousness, as in a splendid robe (Isa. 61:10).

In this way, Jesus Christ, the Son of God and the suffering servant of the Lord, "will bring forth righteousness to the nations" (Isa. 42:1). He brings it to us now, whenever we fall into an imperfection or sin that weighs us down and depresses us, with our own consciences accusing us. He applies his blood afresh to our wounded hearts through the sacrament of reconciliation, and we feel freed indeed, justified anew by his blood poured out in sacrifice for us. Thus he makes us resplendent in his sight, a new creation, sons of the light and of the day, new creatures in Jesus Christ our Lord.

Believe in the Lord Jesus,
and You Will Be Saved

"And wherever he came, in villages, cities, or country, they laid the sick in the market places, and besought him that they might touch even the fringe of his garment; and as many as touched it were saved."
(Mark 6:56)

We see here that Jesus has the power to save. All those who touched "the fringe of his garment ... were saved" (Mark 6:56). The word "saved" means here "were made well," but it is the same Greek word that Christians in the New Testament used to indicate that in Jesus Christ there is salvation, and that all who believe in him will be saved. The Philippian jailer, for example, asked Paul and Silas, "Men, what must I do to be saved? And they said, Believe in the Lord Jesus, and you will be saved, you and your household" (Acts 16:30–31). And Cornelius had a vision of a man named Peter, who "will declare to you a message by which you will be saved, you and all your household" (Acts 11:14). It is the same Greek word "saved" that is used in all three passages.

Jesus Christ came into the world for our salvation, and he performed miracles as signs that he had the power to save us. His cures were signs of something more profound and more important: our salvation. In him we have the salvation that we need and seek. If the Philippian jailer believes in the Lord Jesus Christ, he will be saved; and if the friends of Cornelius believe in Jesus Christ, they will be saved.

Jesus Christ, through faith in him, saves us from our sins and from the depression caused by our guilt. Jesus Christ saves us from eternal punishment in everlasting flames (Matt. 25:41) for our sins because he suffered for us, freeing us from our sins and their punishment, and cleansing our consciences from the pain of guilt.

Christ, through our faith in him, thus gives us a new, radiant, and justified life, in which we can live happily before God, clothed in the splendid righteousness of Jesus Christ himself and sanctified by his blood. We walk in the splendor of his resurrection as new creatures, in a new creation (2 Cor. 5:17; Rev. 21:5; Gal. 6:15), as new men in Jesus Christ (Eph. 4:22–24). He furthermore gives us from the Father the gift of the Holy Spirit so that we might henceforth walk according to the Spirit, and no longer according to the flesh. This is the meaning of being saved in Jesus Christ even now in this present life.

Being saved is having a life that is truly new and illuminated by Jesus Christ. It is to live for him alone who saved us, and doing so with all the love of our hearts (Mark 12:30), with undivided hearts in our love for him, with hearts not divided by the delights of this world, because we have risen with him and even ascended to sit with him in the heavenly places (Eph. 2:6), seeking no longer the things of this world but rather those of above, where Christ is seated at the right hand of God (Col. 3:1–2). This is the meaning of being saved through faith in Jesus Christ.

The Benefits of Faith

"Thomas answered him, My Lord and my God! Jesus said to
him, Have you believed because you have seen me? Blessed are
those who have not seen and yet believed."
(John 20:28–29)

St. Thomas the apostle doubted that Jesus rose from the dead, but after
seeing him, believed and confessed his faith in an extraordinary way,
saying, "My Lord and my God!" (John 20:29).

How important it is to have deep faith like that of St. Thomas. He
had to see Jesus Christ risen from the dead to be able to believe so deeply.
But it is not necessary to see the risen Christ in order to believe in him
and receive all the benefits of faith. In fact, "Blessed," says Jesus, "are
those who have not seen and yet believed" (John 20:29). We are those
people. We can have the same benefits of faith even without seeing him
risen from the dead with our bodily eyes. St. Peter also speaks of this,
saying that "Without having seen him you love him; though you do
not now see him you believe in him and rejoice with unutterable and
exalted joy. As the outcome of your faith you obtain the salvation of
your souls" (1 Pet. 1:8–9).

Through faith, we enter into a relationship with Jesus Christ, whom
we love, and who loves us, and we grow in his love, fed daily by him. It
is Jesus Christ who is the Lamb of God, who takes away our sins and
puts his heavenly peace in our heart, illuminating us from within with
his splendor, with which he shines in our hearts (2 Cor. 4:6). It is he who
saves us by taking our sins from us and bearing them himself—including
the sin of Adam—expiating them by his death on the cross.

Jesus Christ manifests that God is just in forgiving our sins, for with
his own blood, he expiated them, suffering their just punishment for

us and instead of us in order to free us from this alienation from God, saving us from God's wrath by absorbing this wrath into himself on the cross. Thus we see the infinite justice of God in requiring the blood of his own Son in payment of the penalty for the remission of our sins. But this is a justice that is infinitely merciful, for it is God himself, in the person of the Son, who pays our debt for us.

All this happens for us if we have faith and are truly born again in Jesus Christ. We are new creatures (2 Cor. 5:17) with the life and love of God in us. And how happy we are if we also live in accord with the will of God, always doing what he guides us to do! This life of faith and obedience is a truly new life; and we are made new creatures through our faith in Jesus Christ and through his sacraments, which he gave us in order to become truly new, living in his light, peace, and love. When God forgives us and clothes us with the splendor of Jesus Christ, we rejoice from the depth of our hearts and souls—even without having seen him in the flesh—rejoicing "with unutterable and exalted joy" (1 Pet. 1:8).

The Father's Mercy

"And he arose and came to his father. But while he was yet at
a distance, his father saw him and had compassion, and ran
and embraced him and kissed him."
(Luke 15:20)

This important parable of the prodigal son teaches us the love and mercy that God the Father has toward sinners. There are some who think that the Father is just and strict but not merciful. They believe that it was the sacrifice of Jesus Christ that made him change and become merciful. But this is not true. Jesus teaches us in this parable that the Father himself is merciful and full of love for sinners and wants to save them and forgive their sins. The father of the prodigal son represents God the Father. He "had compassion" when he saw his wayward son returning, "and ran and embraced him and kissed him" (Luke 15:20). And not only that, but he also fully restored him as his son and gave a party for him to welcome him home. "The father said to his servants, Bring quickly the best robe, and put it on him; and put a ring on his hand, and shoes on his feet; and bring the fatted calf and kill it, and let us eat and make merry" (Luke 15:22–23).

This is God the Father! He does the same thing to us when we have sinned and then come to him in repentance. And how does he do it? He does it by sending his only Son—who is one being with him in essence, will, and, mind—so that he might make satisfaction on the cross for our sins, so that the Father might be able to justly forgive us for our sins since they have been properly expiated and their penalty duly paid by Christ on the cross. That is, God himself has such love for us that, in the person of his only Son, he satisfies himself that justice has been done in his Son's death on the cross for our sins. Thus, God satisfied his own wrath against sin to be able to justly justify us and forgive our sins. The price had to be paid, and he paid it himself! This is mercy and love in the extreme! God himself suffered our punishment for our sins, for us and instead of us, in order to be able to *justly* forgive us. This is how God acts. The initiative comes from God the Father.

Therefore, the sinner should not be afraid of God the Father. God comes to us in the person of his Son to die on the cross for the remission of our sins. All we need to do is return to God through Jesus Christ in repentance, and he will absolve us through the merits of his death on the cross.

Let us then return to him who says, "If you forgive the sins of any, they are forgiven" (John 20:23). Christ gave to his apostles and to their successors the power to forgive sins, that is, the power to sacramentally channel the merits of his death on the cross and to apply them individually and personally to sinners when they confess their sins.

The Good Fruit of Our Justification by Faith

"And the King will answer them, 'Truly, I say to you, as you did it to one of the least of these my brethren, you did it to me.'"
(Matt. 25:40)

Here Jesus teaches us that when we help a needy person, we help Jesus Christ himself: "As you did it to one of the least of these my brethren, you did it to me" (Matt. 25:40). This is a great revelation. How much we desire to concretely express our love for Jesus Christ! And here he shows us a way of doing it. We can no longer see Christ since his ascension, but if we love him in our brother—who is any person, especially he who is in need—then, Jesus says, we are loving Jesus Christ himself! He said, "Whoever receives one such child in my name receives me" (Matt. 18:5). In receiving and loving anyone in need, we receive and love Jesus Christ. Here, then, we see the foundation for all charitable works and Christian ministry. Whom are we serving and loving in our works of charity and in our ministry of the word? We are helping and loving Jesus Christ himself, and this is how he receives our ministry and charitable works.

We should make a greater effort, therefore, to help others with our gifts. Try every day to help a new person, if you can. Try every day to preach a word of life, salvation, and faith to someone new. We are to jeopardize ourselves and risk being rejected in doing this, in trying to preach to more and more people, in trying to do good to ever new people.

In this gospel reading, we see the importance of good works as the fruit of our faith. Jesus is teaching those who believe in him and is teaching us the fruit that our faith in him should bear if it is genuine and living faith. If our faith does not bear this kind of fruit, it is not genuine and living faith, and it will not save us. Our faith will be known by its fruit. "You will know them by their fruits," Jesus said (Matt. 7:16). "So, every sound tree bears good fruit" (Matt. 7:17). If it does not bear good fruit, it is not a good tree.

We do not justify ourselves through our works, for "a man is justified by faith apart from works of law" (Rom. 3:28). It is only the death of Jesus Christ on the cross that justifies us when we believe in him, for he bore in himself our sins and suffered their punishment on the cross, thereby freeing us from the punishment of eternal death and guilt and clothing us with his own splendid righteousness. Thus, God both pronounces and *makes* us righteous, not through our works but through our faith in Jesus Christ, and thus are we born again and made a new creation (2 Cor. 5:17). And to the degree that we bear good fruit in good works of charity for our needy brethren, to that degree we will grow in sanctification, which God continues to work in us. We rejoice, therefore, in our justification by faith by bearing good fruit in our works of charity for our brethren—and our brother is any person in need.

In the Cross Is Life

"But far be it from me to glory except in the cross of our Lord Jesus Christ, by which the world has been crucified to me, and I to the world." (Gal. 6:14)

When the light is more and more being vanquished by darkness, we celebrate the Exaltation of the Holy Cross, "which drove away darkness and brought in the light" (St. Andrew of Crete, *Breviary*). As the cross is lifted up against the darkening sky, leaving sin and the world behind, so are we lifted up above the world and sin in being crucified with Christ, in order to gain the things that are above (ibid.).

We die to the world with Christ by means of the cross. As darkness increases each day, all of nature dies around us and is incredibly beautiful in its death, with brilliant shades of every color in the leaves falling all about us. So are we too our most beautiful as we die to this mortal world in the death of Jesus Christ on the cross. The cross gives us life and beautifies us as we die on it to the world. St. Paul says that he is dead to the world—crucified to the world—and the world to him through the cross. But as we lose our life in this world for Christ, we save it for God (Mark 8:35). As we hate our life in this world, being crucified to the world with Christ, we keep it for eternal life (John 12:25).

Through the cross, Christ died to this life and saved us. He then wants us to follow the same path, dying to the world with him, being *crucified* to the world with him. "I have been crucified with Christ," says St. Paul (Gal. 2:20). Christ taught us that we are to take this path when he said, "If anyone would come after me, let him deny himself and take up his cross daily and follow me" (Luke 9:23). This is the path of life, a beautiful and narrow path that few find (Matt. 7:13–14). It is the path of "the world being crucified to me, and I to the world" (Gal. 6:14).

By the wood of the cross, Christ saved us from death, which is our punishment for sin. He suffered this punishment for us, in our place, dying on the cross. Freed, then, from death by the cross, we are invited to take up the cross and die to the world, to live henceforth only for him who died for us (2 Cor. 5:15). The cross is the path of life. It saves us from death and shows us the way to live as people saved by Christ. We are to live, dead with him to the world, and the world dead—crucified—to us, that we might henceforth live only for him that died for us (2 Cor. 5:15).

To die to the world is beautiful. We die to all that divides our hearts from a pure and complete, undivided and nuptial love of God. In dying on the cross, Christ brought us eternal life and opened the gates of heaven. This, then, has become the beautiful path of the saints, who died to this world, to live only for God. We are invited to follow their example and take this path of life.

If We Die with Him, We Shall also Live with Him

"Let us lie in wait for the righteous man, because he is inconvenient to us and opposes our actions; he reproaches us for sins against the law, and accuses us of sins against our training … He became a reproof to our thoughts; the very sight of him is a burden to us, because his manner of life is unlike that of others, and his ways are strange."
(Wis. 2:12, 14–15)

This was the experience of Jesus Christ, and he predicts it, saying, "The Son of Man will be delivered into the hands of men, and they will kill him; and when he is killed, after three days he will rise" (Mark 9:31). Jesus prophesied his passion in accord with the typology of the righteous man in the second chapter of the book of Wisdom. In his passion, Jesus fulfilled this Old Testament type and thereby saved us. This persecution of the just man in the passion and death of Jesus Christ gave us new life. His suffering gave us joy in the depth of our spirit, freeing us from our sins by dying for them. He then gave us jubilation of spirit in his resurrection and a life that is completely different and new, a life that is already risen ahead of time and even ascended (Eph 2:6) with the risen and ascended Christ. It is a life that seeks the things that are above, and no longer those of the earth (Col. 3:1–2).

The basis of this new life is the new reconciliation with God that God gives us through the death and resurrection of his only Son, Jesus Christ. In this death, our sins are erased; and in his resurrection, we have this new life that we are now living through our faith in him. It is our faith that communicates these effects to us. But our renewal comes not from our faith but from the death of Jesus Christ, which reconciled

God with us, enabling him to forgive us. Without the death of Jesus Christ, God could not forgive us, for he is God, and God is just, and a just God cannot do such an unjust thing, namely forgive gratuitously and without punishment people who are guilty of grave sins. But the death of his Son, which God himself planned, changed everything and reconciled God to us. This is God's own plan in his eternal love for us, to reconcile himself with us. He planned that his Son should undergo the just punishment necessary for a just God to be able to forgive us in a way that is worthy and appropriate for God, namely in a *just* way. And this is what he does to us now, giving us, in the death of Jesus Christ, all this joy that we now experience in being completely—and *justly*—forgiven, renewed, reconciled with God, and even made participants in a new life in the light of the resurrection of Jesus Christ from the dead.

Renewed and reconciled with God through the death of his Son, we ourselves should now participate in this death, as St. Paul says, "Now I rejoice in my sufferings for your sake, and in my flesh I complete what is lacking in Christ's afflictions for the sake of his body, that is, the Church" (Col. 1:24). His afflictions were his persecutions and the other sufferings of his life of faith. We have to be crucified together with Christ. "I have been crucified with Christ," says St. Paul (Gal. 2:20), and "if we have died with Christ, we believe that we shall also live with him" (Rom. 6:8), and "if we endure, we shall also reign with him" (2 Tim. 2:12).

The experience of the righteous man in the book of Wisdom will become our experience too, as Christians, if we are faithful to Christ in our way of living. They will say to us too that we are inconvenient to them, that we oppose their actions and plans, and that we reproach them for their sins against the law. They will say that we are a reproof of their thoughts, that the very sight of us is a burden to them, that our manner of life is unlike that of others, and that our ways are strange (Wis. 2:12, 14–15).

This is how our lives as Christians will be if we are faithful. We will be criticized, persecuted, and rejected in this world. If we renounce the world and its false and worldly values, the world will reject us as people whose ways are strange and whose manner of life is unlike that of others (see Wis. 2:15). Because we are not of the world, the world will hate us. "If you *were* of the world, the world would love its own; but because you are not of the world, but I chose you out of the world, therefore the world hates you," Jesus said (John 15:19). About his followers, Jesus said, "The world has hated them because they are not of the world, even as I am not of the world" (John 17:14).

This, then, is our life—renewed, forgiven, and full of happiness for the reconciliation we now have with God through the death of his Son. It is a life already risen with him ahead of time, which now seeks the things that are above, and no longer the things of the earth (Col. 3:1–2). Because it is a life the world can no longer understand or accept, it will always be persecuted and rejected in this world.

Thus do we live the mystery of the passion of Jesus Christ. We are participants in his passion. We fulfill, like St. Paul, "what is lacking in Christ's afflictions, for the sake of his body, that is the Church" (Col. 1:24). We are crucified with Christ (Gal. 2:20). We die with him (2 Tim. 2:11) and follow him, carrying our cross (Luke 9:23). This is our glory, and it will bring us to the resurrection and the fullness of life.

A Witness of the Resurrection

"So one of the men who have accompanied us during all the time
that the Lord Jesus went in and out among us, beginning from the
baptism of John until the day when he was taken up from us—one of
these men must become with us a witness to his resurrection."
(Acts 1:21–22)

St. Matthias was one of the disciples of Jesus that lived with him and
saw him risen (1 Cor. 15:5–7). He was therefore elected after the ascension, but before Pentecost, to be a witness with the eleven to the
resurrection of Jesus Christ.

The resurrection of Jesus Christ from the dead was an important
part of the proclamation of the faith, the proclamation of the salvation
of God through the death and resurrection of Jesus Christ for all who
believe in him.

All need this salvation because no one is righteous, no one has lived
perfectly according to the law of God (Rom. 3:10). All are therefore
cursed by the law, which says, "Cursed be he who does not confirm the
words of this law by doing them" (Deut. 27:26). The gentiles had the
moral law of God written on their hearts (Rom. 1:19–21; 2:15), but
they did not keep it (Rom. 1:21–22), and so they are "without excuse"
(Rom. 1:20), just as are the Jews, and hence, "as it is written," as St. Paul
says, "None is righteous, no, not one; no one understands, no one seeks
for God. All have turned aside, together they have gone wrong; no one
does good, not even one" (Rom. 3:10–12; Ps. 14:1–3).

Everyone, therefore, Jews as well as Gentiles, needs God's salvation,
which he sent into the world in his Son, Jesus Christ, through his death
for our sins on the cross and through his resurrection, which shows that
his death was effective and accepted by God for the remission of our

sins, through his substitution for us in bearing our just penalty on the cross.

The apostles preached this victory of Jesus Christ over death. We do not have to die eternally if we believe in Christ, because he died for us, remitting our sins, and rose victorious over death, introducing a new kind of life, the life of the resurrection, which we can now have in his resurrection. It is a resplendent life, illuminated by the light streaming from his resurrection.

So we rise with him to a new and risen life, having died with him to our sins through his death, which paid our debt for our sins and thus freed us for this new and resplendent life in his resurrection.

St. Matthias joined the eleven to live and preach this. We too live and preach this salvation of God in Jesus Christ, dead and risen.

Newness of Life

"Of this man's posterity God has brought to Israel a Savior."
(Acts 13:23)

We are, in these readings from Acts, in the first days of early Christianity, after the resurrection, and we hear the first recorded sermon of St. Paul, given in the synagogue of Antioch in Pisidia, in present-day southern Turkey.

St. Paul briefly recounts what God has done to save his people throughout their history, until he "brought to Israel a Savior" (Acts 13:23). The Jews, he says, killed him, but God raised him from the dead. He concludes, saying, "Be it known unto you, therefore, men and brethren, that through this man is preached unto you the forgiveness of sins: And by him all that believe are justified from all things, from which ye could not be justified by the law of Moses" (Acts 13:38–39 KJV).

Such was the primitive preaching about Christ—dead and risen—in whom is forgiveness, justification, and salvation for "all that believe" (Acts 13:39). The experience of those first days after the resurrection was one of interior renovation through faith in Jesus Christ, dead and risen. They are dead with him to their sins and risen with him for a new life in his resurrection. Through faith in him, his death destroyed their sins, and his resurrection gave them a new, illuminated, and risen life.

St. Paul told them that they could not be justified before God through the law. This was because no one could keep the law perfectly. They were, therefore, always guilty before God as far as keeping the law was concerned (Deut. 27:26). Only Jesus Christ satisfied the law for them, bearing its curse and punishment for them (Deut. 27:26; Gal. 3:13; Deut. 21:23). Only he perfectly fulfilled it, without sin, and only he satisfied the justice of God in suffering the punishment of the law on their behalf as their new covenant head or representative, dying for them on the cross. The law and all its requirements are, therefore, fulfilled for them in Jesus Christ if they believe in him. And his resurrection shows forth the results, namely that they can now walk in "newness of life" (Rom. 6:4), and live in the Spirit (Rom. 8:9), risen with Christ (Col. 3:1–2), with him shining in their hearts (2 Cor. 4:6).

No one achieved this justification through the law. The law was too difficult for them and only multiplied their sins and increased their guilt in not being able to keep it. But now, through faith in Christ, dead and risen, this guilt is removed from our hearts, and our debt of disobedience is paid by Christ on the cross, taking our punishment, and suffering it for us and instead of us, thus freeing us to walk in newness of life in the light of his resurrection.

Such was the new life and joy of the early days of Christianity, and it is our joy too through our faith in Jesus Christ, in whom we have a new and illuminated life in peace with God.

The Good Shepherd

"I am the good shepherd.
The good shepherd lays down his life for the sheep."
(John 10:11)

During the beautiful time of Easter, we meditate on the image of Jesus Christ the good shepherd, who lays down his life for his sheep. We are his sheep, and he gives his life for us, so that we might live *through* him and draw life from him (John 1:16). "In this the love of God was made manifest among us, that God sent his only Son into the world, so that we might live *through* him" (1 John 4:9). He is our life. We are in him, and he lives in us. We are to live *through* him. *In* him we have the fullness of life.

He gave his life to be able to be in us. He gave us his sacramentalized body and blood in the Eucharist so that we might e at him and thus live in him, and he in us. He wants us to live in him and through him. "Because I live," he says, "you will live also" (John 14:19). We draw life from him (John 1:16), the life of God, which he gave us. "As the living Father sent me, and as I live because of the Father," he said, "so he who eats me will live because of me" (John 6:57).

As a good shepherd, Jesus Christ has given his life for his sheep. We draw life from him, from his fullness (John 1:16), and so we remain in his love, as he remains in his Father's love (John 15:9). As Christ lives through the Father, drawing life from him, so we live through Christ, drawing life from Christ, and we live in his love. In this way, we draw our new life in the Spirit through Christ.

Christ gave his life for us by offering himself as a sacrifice of love to his Father. This uniquely adequate sacrifice of himself, as the only Son of God, saved us and reconciled us with the Father. As a result, the risen Christ then sent from the Father the Holy Spirit to renew us and fill our hearts with the love of God (Rom. 5:5).

How much we need the Holy Spirit and the Eucharist, which is the body and blood, person and life of Jesus Christ, with all his love dwelling in our hearts, illumining them! He saves us from our sins and imperfections that sadden us and darken our spirit. He comes to us every day to save us anew from this darkness, illumining us ever anew with his life, love, and his ever new gift of the Holy Spirit, who renews us and rejoices our hearts.

Jesus Christ, who gave his life for us as our good shepherd, justifies us before God, making us new, clean, forgiven, and illuminated. He shines within us and makes us resplendent, clothing us with his own righteousness (Isa. 61:10). And he is the definitive cure for our guilty conscience, for in his death he destroys our guilt for our sins and imperfections.

He gave his life for us to save us from the death of our spirits by propitiating and placating the wrath of God against our sins. His death in substitution for us freed us from the death of our spirits and removed from us the pain and suffering of guilt and the danger of eternal death. In his death, we die to death. His death destroys our eternal death. His death on the cross destroys death for all his elect. The death of Jesus Christ is the death of death.

He therefore rose from the dead on the third day, victorious over death, Satan, and sin. He rose that we might rise new in him to a new life, filled with his love and with the Holy Spirit. In this way we shall remain in his love and walk in the "newness of life" (Rom. 6:4), in the light of his resurrection. As we die with him to our sins, in the same way we rise with him to live a new life, illuminated by his love.

Truly, as St. Peter says, "there is salvation in no one else, for there is no other name under heaven given among men by which we must be saved" (Acts 4:12). Truly, there is no one else who suffered our punishment for us, giving his life for his sheep. He is the only one who has done this, and the only one who could have done this, for only the only begotten Son of God, equal to the Father in divinity, could satisfy divine justice on our behalf, suffering the punishment due for our sins, so that we might be freed from this suffering and from our sins and guilt, and made new and resplendent in God's sight.

Only God could do this for us, renewing us in this way, and he could only do it as a man. God, furthermore, became incarnate as a man only once, for men and women of every nation and religion. There is only *one* only begotten Son of God made man. There has not been another. And he became man for all nations, cultures, and religions. He wants everyone to come to him. This is why he said, "Go ye into all the world, and preach the gospel to every creature" (Mark 16:15 KJV). We therefore preach the gospel to everyone so that all might have the opportunity to be saved and come to a new life in him with their sins forgiven and their guilt removed.

Jesus Christ, our good shepherd, said, "No one comes to the Father, but by me" (John 14:6). Indeed, he is the way, the truth, and the life, and no one comes to the Father except by him. He gave his life for us so that we might go to the Father through him. "I lay down my life for the sheep," he says (John 10:15). Let us therefore come to him who is our good shepherd.

Christ Calms the Storms in Our Hearts

"And he awoke and rebuked the wind, and said to the sea,
Peace! Be still! And the wind ceased, and there was a great calm."
(Mark 4:39)

Jesus calms the wind and the sea, and they obey him. This is important for us because it is the same Jesus Christ who died, rose from the dead, ascended into heaven, and is seated at the right hand of the Father, who calms our hearts and gives us interior peace in the midst of the storms that arise within us. This episode in the boat symbolizes for us what Jesus Christ does in our hearts.

How easy it is to lose our peace and experience a storm in our hearts by falling into an imperfection! God allows us to experience this in order to move us to avoid this imperfection in the future and thus grow in holiness and in a life of perfection. Yet at the same time, he gives us the remedy for our suffering and for the pain in our hearts. The remedy is Jesus Christ himself, who died and rose for us. By calling upon him, invoking the merits of his death on the cross, he stands for us before the Father to absorb the Father's just, holy, and necessary wrath against us for our sins, instead suffering it himself on the cross. Thus, the necessary wrath of God is expressed against us for having done wrong, but at the same time, it is absorbed for us by the Son of God on the cross, to free us from this suffering, from this pain of heart, from this guilt, from this storm in our hearts, and from the fear of eternal death, in case of serious sin. And so God, through Jesus Christ, calms the storm in our hearts and gives us great peace. This happens through our faith and prayer when we ask it of Christ, because for this he suffered on the cross, to place himself between us and the Father in order to absorb our just punishment and the divine wrath, justly directed against us.

This is why Jesus established the sacraments, particularly the sacrament of reconciliation (Matt. 18:18; John 20:23), so that through this sacrament, we might be able to experience in a personal way the mediatory work of Christ on the cross and receive genuine relief from the pain in our hearts, caused by our imperfections or sins, and so see the storm in our hearts changed into a great calm. Christ wants his forgiveness, through his work on the cross, to be a real experience in our hearts. For this reason, he gave us this sacrament that is so psychologically effective and satisfying. He knows our psychological needs, and so this is how he deals with us. Christ wanted the merits of his suffering on the cross to be personally and individually applied to us in a way that would be psychologically effective. So he left us the sacrament of reconciliation whereby he channels these merits to us.

When this happens, it is as though all things have been made new, for "if anyone be in Christ, he is a new creature: old things are passed away; behold, all things are become new," as St. Paul affirms (2 Cor. 5:17). So does God renew us, and so do we grow little by little in holiness. All this works through faith. We always have to call upon Jesus Christ in every new storm. We are never independent but rather always dependent upon him who died and rose for us so that we might live for him.

Saved by Faith

"An evil and adulterous generation seeks for a sign; but no sign shall
be given to it except the sign of the prophet Jonah."
(Matt. 12:39)

Asking Jesus for a sign was itself a sign of their lack of faith in him,
which the scribes and Pharisees should have had after seeing so many
miracles, healings, and signs. It was, in other words, a refusal to believe when they had already been given sufficient evidence. Instead of
requesting still another sign, they should simply have believed in him
to experience his salvation. But Jesus does promise them yet one more
sign, his resurrection, which should convince all of good will. He said,
"For as Jonah was three days and three nights in the belly of the whale,
so will the Son of Man be three days and three nights in the heart of
the earth" (Matt. 12:40).

Jesus then gave them two examples of faith: that of the Queen of
the South, and that of the Ninevites in the days of Jonah. These are
both examples of pagans that had more faith than the Jewish scribes
and Pharisees, who were requesting still another sign from Jesus after
they had seen so many. The pagans of Nineveh, says, Jesus, "will arise at
the judgment with this generation and condemn it; for they repented
at the preaching of Jonah, and something greater than Jonah is here,"
yet they do not believe in him (Matt. 12:41). And the Queen of the
South came to hear Solomon, and "something greater than Solomon is
here," yet they refuse to believe in him (Matt. 12:42). While even Pagans
believed in Solomon and Jonah, the religious leaders of the Jews refuse
to believe in the Messiah himself! What lack of faith in those that we
should most expect to find faith!

And where are you in all of this? You have even seen the greatest sign of all, promised here by Jesus: his resurrection. Do you truly believe in him as your Savior who can save you as he saved the Israelites from the Egyptians in the Red Sea? Moses said to them, "Fear not, stand firm, and see the salvation of the Lord, which he will work for you today … The Lord will fight for you, and you have only to be still" (Exod. 14:13–14).

This is the salvation that God will work for you, through Jesus Christ, when you believe in him and entreat his help, especially through his sacraments. He will free you from the Egyptians, who for us are the devil and his followers, eternal death in hell, sin, and spiritual death, which is the result of sin. This is why Jesus Christ came into the world, to give you this freedom and salvation if you believe in him and live from now on for him alone with all your heart. He will give you his light and enable you walk with him in light. He will forgive you for your sins and imperfections and give you new life. You will rise with him to live a new and risen life (Rom. 6:4), lived for him alone, in his light, with a clear and clean conscience and with God's joy in your heart. Thus does he wish you to live—in his light, not in the darkness and sadness of sin (John 8:12; 12:46). You should then leave behind your old worldly life and rise and even ascend with him to a risen and ascended life (Eph. 2:6; Col. 2:12). But for this to happen, you must believe in the power of his blood, which paid the debt of punishment for your sins, and invoke it, and then rise with him to new life in his resurrection (Rom. 6:4; Col. 3:1–2). This is what he promises to those who have faith in him.

The Harvest of the Earth

"So it will be at the close of the age. The angels will come out and separate the evil from the righteous, and throw them into the furnace of fire, where there will be wailing and gnashing of teeth."
(Matt. 13:49–50)

We are now awaiting the end of the world when "the angels will come out and separate the evil from the righteous" (Matt. 13:49). In mid-summer, the fruits of the earth are ripening for the harvest. The harvest of the earth is the great symbol of the final harvest of the world, at the end of the age, when the angels, the reapers, will come out and separate the weeds from the wheat and cast the weeds into the fire and put the wheat into the barn. The fire is the eternal fire of hell, "where there will be wailing and gnashing of teeth" (Matt. 13:42), and the barn full of wheat is the fullness of the kingdom of God. We now await this day of judgment, a day of fire and light—fire for "the sons of the evil one" and light for "the sons of the kingdom" (Matt. 13:38)—for "then the righteous will shine like the sun in the kingdom of their Father" (Matt. 13:43).

"So it will be at the close of the age. The angels will come out and separate the evil from the righteous" (Matt. 13:49). They will cast the wicked "into the furnace of fire, where there will be wailing and gnashing of teeth" (Matt. 13:50). It will be like a net full of fish, which the fishermen drag ashore … putting the good ones into baskets and throwing the bad ones away (Matt. 13:48).

God would like to gather everyone, and so he throws the net into the sea, but he also knows that not all will be good and worthy of the kingdom of God. It is up to us, then, to receive the justification of Christ with faith so that God, through sending his Son as a substitute for us on the cross, absorbing in this way his righteous wrath against our sins, can justly forgive us. He then clothes us with the righteousness of Christ himself (Isa. 61:10) when we believe in him and invoke the merits of his death on the cross. And so we shine even now with the righteousness of Jesus Christ. Then we must cooperate with the grace of God and try to obey him in everything so that we might be sanctified. Only those who are justified and sanctified will be chosen and put into baskets at the end of the age. The angels will cast the rest into the furnace of fire.

We are now awaiting this day of glory and light, clothing ourselves with the righteousness of Jesus Christ, living from his resurrection. But this present life is also a school in which God is always teaching us new things, punishing us in our hearts for our errors, imperfections, and sins, so that we will learn and be prepared and perfected on the last day to be among the elect, who will shine like the sun in the kingdom of our Father.

Part III:
Salvation and Divinization through Christ's Incarnation, Death, Resurrection, and the Eucharist

Assurance of Final Perseverance

"Jesus said to her, I am the resurrection and the life; he who believes in me, though he die, yet shall he live, and whoever lives and believes in me shall never die."
(John 11:25–26

Jesus raised Lazarus after he was four days in the sepulcher to reveal his glory and to demonstrate that he has the power to give eternal life to us who believe in him. In the resurrection of Lazarus, we see that Jesus Christ has power over death, and his word to Martha explains this power, showing its importance for all who believe in him.

If we believe in Jesus Christ, although we all die in the body, we will live with him in the spirit, that is, we will continue to live, and on the last day we will rise in our bodies to live with him in his kingdom forever. Eternal death will not touch those who believe in him. They are destined for life, not for death. He will give those who believe in him the gift of final perseverance. He has the power to assure the final perseverance of the saints who believe in him, and he also has the power to assure them that they will persevere to the end. Not everyone knows this assurance, and it is not necessary for salvation, but many of the saints do enjoy this special gift of assurance of final perseverance, the assurance that they are among the elect, predestined for eternal life.

It is Christ who justifies and sanctifies his elect. But they must do their part to be sanctified, and this is the fruit of their justification. They must live a new life in Christ, a new life in the Spirit, and according to the Spirit, not according to the flesh. They must live a life that is an offering to the Father, with and through the sacrifice of Jesus Christ on the cross (Luke 9:23; Col 1:24). We are then united to Christ in his one and only sacrifice of himself, offered to the Father in love, and we make of our life also a living sacrifice, offered with Christ to the Father. Our sanctified life is, therefore, a new and sacrificial life, a eucharistic life, an offering of love, a hymn of praise, offered in the eucharistic sacrifice, the one and only sacrifice of Jesus Christ on Calvary for the salvation of the world.

So Christ assures us of final perseverance, promising eternal life and victory over death to those who believe in him and live according to the Spirit, not according to the flesh, for "those who are in the flesh cannot please God" (Rom. 8:8). To walk according to the Spirit and not according to the flesh is the fruit that shows that we truly believe, and those who really believe will never die. In other words, they are promised the gift of final perseverance—that "whoever lives and believes in me shall never die" (John 11:26). Thus has God predestined us for life. We will never die, for we have already passed over from death to life, and we will not come to the judgment of condemnation (John 5:24).

The resurrection of Lazarus points to this, and the resurrection of Jesus Christ proves it definitively. Crying out with a loud voice, Jesus said to Lazarus in the tomb, "Lazarus, come forth. The dead man came out, his hands and feet bound with bandages and his face wrapped with a cloth. Jesus said to them, Unbind him, and let him go" (John 11:43–44). So also does he do to us. He resurrects us now in the midst of this present, old life and old world, to be the first fruits of the new world of the resurrection, just as Jesus, in rising on the third day, became the first fruits of the resurrection on the last day.

In this present life, we rise ahead of time, through the power of Jesus Christ when we believe in him. He gives us new and risen lives, renewing us interiorly, recreating us, making us a new creation (2 Cor. 5:17), new creatures, new men, dead to sin and alive in the Spirit, to no longer walk according to the disordered desires of the flesh and of the body (Rom. 8:13), but according to the desires of the Spirit.

The Eucharist, the Sacrifice
of the New Testament

"Then they shall take some of the blood, and put it on the two
doorposts and the lintel of the houses in which they eat them ... The
blood shall be a sign for you upon the houses where you are; and
when I see the blood, I will pass over you, and no plague shall fall
upon you to destroy you, when I smite the land of Egypt."
(Exod. 12:7, 13)

Jesus Christ is the paschal lamb of the New Testament. As the passover
lamb was slain by the Israelites in Egypt to free them from the plague
of the death of the firstborn, so Christ was sacrificed for us to free us
from eternal death for our sins. The paschal lamb was slain instead of
the firstborn of the Israelites. It substituted for them. Instead of them,
the lamb suffered the plague of death. Therefore, none of the firstborn
of the Jews died while all the firstborn of the Egyptians died. Wherever the blood of the paschal lamb was smeared, that family was saved
from the plague of death. In the same way, Christ was slain instead of
us sinners, who should have experienced eternal death in hell for our
sins. He substituted for us, dying instead of us. The Father smote him
instead of us, and his poured-out blood saved us from death. Thus, he
reconciled God to us, absorbing his wrath against our sins, in sacrificing himself.

As the Jewish Passover supper is the annual memorial of their salvation from Egypt, so the Eucharist is our memorial of the sacrifice of
Christ, who saved us from death. Christ said, "As often as you eat this
bread and drink the cup, you proclaim the Lord's death until he comes"
(1 Cor. 11:26). In the Eucharist, the bread becomes the immolated body

of Jesus Christ, and the wine becomes his blood poured out in sacrifice. The Lord's Supper, which we continue to celebrate, makes present for us the one and only sacrifice of Jesus Christ on the cross for our salvation. It is Jesus Christ, offered in sacrifice on the cross to the Father. The Eucharist puts us on Calvary at the moment of Christ's sacrifice and makes this one and only sacrifice present for us. The Eucharist does not repeat the one sacrifice of Christ on the cross for our salvation but rather makes this one sacrifice of the New Testament present for us so that we might participate in it and offer it with Christ to the Father for the glory of God and the salvation of the world.

We also are to offer ourselves in this one sacrifice, together with Christ, to the Father, in the Holy Spirit. Then our whole lives should become a sacrifice of love, offered with Christ to the Father, in the Holy Spirit. We are to pour out our lives for our brethren and so walk as Christ walked, for "he who says he abides in him ought to walk in the same way in which he walked" (1 John 2:6). This is because "by this we know love, that he laid down his life for us; and we ought to lay down our lives for the brethren" (1 John 3:16). In doing this, offer ourselves to the Father with Christ in the eucharistic sacrifice.

Jesus gives us an example of this by washing his disciples' feet, saying, "If I then, your Lord and Teacher, have washed your feet, you also ought to wash one another's feet. For I have given you an example, that you also should do as I have done to you" (John 13:14–15).

We then offer our lives of love and service of our brethren in the Eucharist, pouring out our lives in love with Christ to the Father in the Holy Spirit.

The Eucharist Divinizes
the Human Race

"Then he ordered the crowds to sit down on the grass; and taking
the five loaves and the two fish he looked up to heaven, and
blessed, and broke and gave the loaves to the disciples, and the
disciples gave them to the crowds."
(Matt. 14:19)

Jesus miraculously feeds the people in the desert. This is a foretaste
of the Eucharist, in which he feeds us with heavenly bread, which is
his eucharistic body. The Eucharist is bread which comes down from
heaven and gives life to the world (John 6:33). This eucharistic bread is
Jesus Christ himself, who came down to the earth from heaven so that
we might eat his flesh and drink his blood and so live a new life in him,
fed on his body and blood, which contain his divinity.

Christ's divinity became united with his humanity in the incarnation.
His divine person together with his divine nature assumed a human nature with a human mind and a human will so that we could have direct
physical and sacramental contact with God for our transformation and
divinization. In this divinization, though, we, of course, remain human,
even though we are divinized by our contact with the body and blood
of Jesus Christ. In a similar way, the humanity of Jesus remained human even though his human body, human mind, and human will were
divinized by their contact with his divine person with its divine nature.
Yet the divinization of Jesus's humanity was far more intense than our
divinization because of the uniqueness of the hypostatic union uniting
his humanity to his divinity. In short, to be divinized means to be filled

with divinity, to be transformed and illumined from within by contact with God while we remain human.

Jesus Christ, therefore, came to the earth for our divinization. He sacramentalized his human body and blood, which contain his divine person and divine nature, so that in eating his eucharistic body, we can touch God in a physical, sacramental way and be transformed and divinized by this touch, by this contact with divinity.

In the incarnation, the humanity of Jesus Christ was divinized that all humanity might be divinized through its contact with his divinized humanity, Thus the incarnation took place for the divinization of the human race. The human race is made a new creation by means of the incarnation if we have faith in Jesus Christ, are saved and justified by his death, risen with him in his resurrection, and spiritually fed by him in the Eucharist.

The Eucharist is for the transformation of the world because it makes present the expiatory and propitiatory death of Jesus Christ on the cross and puts us into physical, sacramental contact with the divinized and divinizing body of Jesus Christ himself.

The Paschal Mystery

"Thus it is written, that the Christ should suffer and on the third
day rise from the dead, and that repentance and forgiveness of
sins should be preached in his name to all nations."
(Luke 24:46–47)

The mystery of the death and resurrection of Jesus Christ is the paschal mystery, through which our sins are forgiven and we are saved.
This mystery was known and deliberately planned to occur in this way
from before the creation of the world (1 Pet. 1:20). It was not just an
accident or a tragedy that God foreknew and permitted; it was rather
God's own definitive plan for our redemption.

It was not that Jesus only came to teach us and unfortunately got
himself killed in the process. Nor was his death only an example of how
Jesus poured out his life even unto death on a cross out of love for us,
nor was it only meant as an example of how God forgives everything,
even the killing of his own Son, nor was it only meant as an example of
how Jesus, in his great love for us, forgave even those who killed him.

Rather, God planned it in this way, because only through the death
and resurrection of his Son could we be saved, and our sins adequately
be forgiven, expiated, and totally propitiated. Christ's death was not a
tragic accident, but rather the chosen and desired means through which
God could forgive our sins and still remain a righteous and just God
who punishes all sin. St. Peter therefore says, "this Jesus, delivered up
according to the definite plan and foreknowledge of God, you crucified
and killed" (Acts 2:23).

His death was no accident, but was necessary for our salvation, and
God prepared us for it through the prophets, as St. Peter affirms, saying,
"what God foretold by the mouth of all the prophets, that his Christ

should suffer, he thus fulfilled" (Acts 3:18). Jesus himself tells us the same thing, saying, "Thus it is written, that the Christ should suffer and on the third day rise from the dead" (Luke 24:46). His death was the necessary means through which God could justly forgive our sins.

Christ, therefore, died for our sins. "He is the propitiation for our sins," as St. John says (1 John 2:2 KJV). As the propitiation given by God, he satisfied the justice of God and of the law of God on our behalf. He propitiated this justice. He propitiated the righteous, just, holy, and necessary wrath of God against all sin in his death on the cross. He satisfied this necessary justice.

Then, on the third day, he rose from the dead to complete the paschal mystery, the mystery of our salvation. Freed and justly forgiven for our sins in the death of Christ, what will happen to us next? He rose from the dead for this, so that freed from our sins, we might rise with him to a new and risen life.

Hence his death is our death to sin, and his resurrection is our resurrection to a new and risen life. Thus the paschal mystery of the death and resurrection of Jesus Christ completely renews us, and gives us a new life in the Spirit, so that from now on we might live according to the Spirit, and no longer according to the flesh.

We have therefore been given a new kind of life in this world. It is the life of those who have been born again in Jesus Christ. It is a life centered on God and lived only for him. It is, furthermore, a life in which we need to grow much. It is a life in which we are in a long process of sanctification. This means that we have to learn step by step how to live only for God in this world.

Dead therefore in the death of Christ to our sins and risen in his resurrection to a new and risen life, we become new creatures, new men, a new creation in Jesus Christ with a mission to the world. We now have a gospel to preach and an example to give for the salvation of the world, for its transformation through the paschal mystery into the new creation (2 Cor. 5:17; Rev. 21:5).

Joy in the Holy Spirit

"Behold, my servant whom I have chosen, my beloved with
whom my soul is well pleased. I will put my Spirit upon him, and
he shall proclaim justice to the Gentiles."
(Matt. 12:18; Isa. 42:1)

St. Matthew presents Jesus as the fulfillment of the suffering servant of
Isaiah. St. Matthew cites the first of the suffering servant hymns (Isa.
42:1–4). This servant is the beloved of God. God puts his Spirit upon
him, "and he shall proclaim justice to the Gentiles" (Matt. 12:18; Isa.
42:1).

The Jews sought the righteousness of God—that is, they longed to be
righteous and justified by God through faith (Gen. 15:6; Rom. 4:3)
and to grow in holiness through their obedience to his will and their
observance of his law. But the Gentiles would receive this righteousness
directly from the servant of the Lord, Jesus Christ. This servant, then,
would bring the righteousness of God to both Gentiles and Jews, for
he is the fulfillment of God's salvation for all. He justifies the Gentiles
as well as the Jews through his death on the cross and his resurrection
from the dead.

Although the Jews were justified by their faith since the days of Abraham (Gen. 15:6; Rom. 4:3), and their sins were forgiven through their
faith, nonetheless, their sins were not yet justly or properly expiated
until the death of Jesus Christ on the cross. God only forgave them
with the intention of properly expiating their sins later through the
death of his Son (Rom. 3:25–26). Jesus Christ is, therefore, the Savior
of the Jews too, and now, with him present with them in the flesh, they
have the fullness of God's salvation with them, and in his resurrection,
they can rise with him to a new and risen life. Hence the Jews can now

hope in this Savior along with the Gentiles, as the text says, "and in his name will the Gentiles hope" (Matt. 12:21). The coming of Jesus was the first announcement of salvation to the Gentiles, "and he shall proclaim justice to the Gentiles" (Matt. 12:18). From then on, all have salvation in Jesus Christ—Jews as well as Gentiles.

This salvation is something interior. It is the cleansing of the conscience that gives us joy of spirit, the happiness of God in our heart: "For the kingdom of God does not mean food and drink but righteousness and peace and joy in the Holy Spirit" (Rom. 14:17). To have our sins forgiven and to have the new life of God shining in our hearts is something interior. The Savior will therefore be gentle. "He will not wrangle or cry aloud, nor will any one hear his voice in the streets; he will not break a bruised reed or quench a smoldering wick, till he brings justice to victory" (Matt. 12:19–20). He will be a gentle and benevolent Savior, and in him, we will find the happiness of God, which we so yearn for. He will bring justice to victory, that is, he will bring his righteousness and salvation, which justifies and renews us, illuminating us with new life and happiness in the Lord.

Transformed by the Death, Resurrection, and Eucharistic Presence of Jesus Christ

"Was it not necessary that the Christ should suffer these things and
enter into his glory?"
(Luke 24:26)

It is a new world, a new era in the history of mankind in which we now live because of the resurrection into eschatological glory of Jesus Christ, now, ahead of time, in the midst of history. His resurrection inaugurates the community of the final days, which is the Church. The blessings proper to the last days are now already present in the community that believes in Jesus Christ risen from the dead.

The members of this community are also risen in him (Col. 2:12; 3:1–2) and walk in his splendor. They are remade into a new creation in him through their faith. Their sins are erased by him, and they walk already in the liberty of the children of God, illuminated within their hearts by him. Christ is the one who now shines in their hearts with the illumination of God (2 Cor. 4:6), changing them "from glory to glory" in his own image by the action of the Holy Spirit (2 Cor. 3:18).

Therefore, they walk in the light. Their guilt has been erased by the merits of Christ's death on the cross because he "redeemed us from the curse of the law, having become a curse for us—for it is written, Cursed be everyone who hangs on a tree" (Gal. 3:13; Deut. 21:23). Thus he bought us back as slaves in order to liberate us from our slavery to sin and guilt; and the price he paid to buy us back and free us was his own blood poured out on the cross. He became a curse before God by being hanged on a tree (Deut. 21:23) in order to free us from the curse due to us because of our sins. That is, he assumed onto himself the curse that we bore because of our sins, and in being crucified in punishment for these sins, he set us free from this curse. Thus "you were ransomed from the futile ways ... not with perishable things such as silver or gold, but with the precious blood of Christ, like that of a lamb without blemish or spot" (1 Pet. 1:18–19).

We rise with Christ as a result of his redemption. Washed by the blood of Christ (Eph. 2:13), which was shed to redeem us from sin when the Son of God died in our place as the precious lamb of sacrifice, we are now freed from our guilt to live a new and risen life in him (Col. 3:1–2). We are, therefore, to walk in the newness of life (Rom 6:4), in the light of the risen Christ (Jn 8:12), enjoying the liberty of the children of God (Rom. 8:21).

Two of Jesus's disciples were discovering all of this little by little as they walked to Emmaus with the risen Christ, who explained to them that truly it was "necessary that the Christ should suffer these things and enter into his glory" (Luke 24:26). Without suffering these things, he would not have redeemed us. In his death is our death to sin. Through his sacrifice, we are saved; and in his resurrection, we enjoy a new life, a new quality of life, the life of a new creature (2 Cor. 5:17), living in a new creation, for "Behold, I make all things new," said the risen Lord (Rev. 21:5).

Then the eyes of those two disciples were opened in the breaking of the bread with the risen Christ. And this is what happens in every Eucharist. Christ makes himself present in the bread and wine, which are transformed into his body and blood, sacrificed on the altar for our redemption from sin.

What happens on the altar is that "the Lamb of God who takes away the sin of the world" (John 1:29) becomes a curse, or is cursed, for the Eucharist is the sacrifice of Calvary made present for us, where Christ was cursed by being hung upon a tree (Deut. 21:23; Gal. 3:13). In the Eucharist, we are made present at Calvary at the moment of the sacrifice of Jesus Christ, in which he suffered for our sins, freeing us from all guilt.

Christ's sacrifice infinitely pleased God, for it was an act of love by God's own divine Son, in which the Son freely offered himself to God for us. In his death, Christ accepted our guilt upon himself and suffered its just penalty, thereby fulfilling the requisites of divine justice and freeing us from eternal death as well as from spiritual death.

Then we eat his body and drink his blood, uniting ourselves to him, the eternal Word, and we recognize him in the breaking of the bread. He feeds and fills us with his divinity because his body and blood are singularly divinized by the person of the Word.

We are thus redeemed by his death, justified and illuminated by his resurrection, and fed and divinized by his body and blood. This is the new creation, wrought by the death and resurrection of Jesus Christ.

The Eucharistic Christ Sanctifies, Illuminates, and Renews the World

"Jesus then took the loaves, and when he had given thanks, he distributed them to those who were seated."
(John 6:11)

Jesus feeds five thousand men with five loaves and two fish. He gives thanks over the bread and distributes it among the people. Then, in the gospel of John, there follows a long discourse on the bread of life, the bread that comes down from heaven and gives life to the world. Jesus himself is this bread of life. The living bread is his body and blood. This entire chapter of St. John's gospel is about the Eucharist, for in the Eucharist, Jesus feeds us miraculously with the bread of life, that is, with himself, with his eucharistic flesh and blood. In the Eucharist, we consume Jesus Christ, sacramentalized for the life of the world.

Jesus Christ is the second person of the Blessed Trinity, the eternal Son of the Father, who existed from all eternity in the bosom of the Father. He became incarnate through the work of the Holy Spirit in the Virgin Mary. In the incarnation, his divine person with his divine nature entered into union with a human nature and sanctified it. His humanity and his human body contained his divinity and his divine person here on earth for the transformation of the world. By means of our contact with him in faith, we are transformed and sanctified, instructed and changed.

Jesus Christ justified and saved us by his death on the cross, whereby he paid our debt of punishment and suffering for our sins, thus satisfying divine justice. In the Eucharist, his death on the cross is made present for us so that we can participate in his sacrifice and be freed from the punishment due to our sins. Then, in Holy Communion, we eat the flesh and blood of Jesus Christ that were offered in sacrifice to the Father in substitution for us in order to suffer our punishment for our sins. By eating his flesh and drinking his blood, we eat the flesh and drink the blood of God for our transformation and divinization. Christ's physical body contained his divine person. The Eucharist sacramentalizes his physical body for us in a form that we can eat. We therefore eat the body of Christ which contains his divine person. By taking his divine person into ourselves by eating his sacramentalized body, we are divinized—that is, filled with his divinity. The Eucharist, then, is our food and drink for the life of our souls.

The divine person of Jesus Christ divinizes his humanity, that is, fills it with divinity, even though it always remains a human nature, with a human mind and a human will. Nonetheless, for our salvation, his humanity is full of his divinity, illuminating his humanity from within. God did this for our salvation so that we, who have been justified by his death on the cross through our faith in him, may now also be divinized and grow further by eating and drinking his flesh and blood, which contain for us his divinity. Thus, by receiving Holy Communion with faith, those who are justified by his death can now be sanctified and divinized with his divinity illuminating them from within, just as his divine person illuminated his physical humanity from within and divinized it. As his humanity always remained human, even though divinized, in the same way, we also always remain human, although divinized by eating and drinking the eucharistic body and blood of Jesus Christ. We receive and eat Jesus Christ, sacramentalized in the Eucharist. This is for our illumination and divinization. Thus, the divinity of Jesus Christ illuminates our humanity from within, divinizing it.

The Eucharist is also a sacrifice of praise that we offer to the Father, with the Son, in the Holy Spirit. Christ offers himself to the Father, pouring out his life in love for us, in substitution for us, but also as a sacrifice offered in love and self-gift to the Father. Christ's sacrifice of himself in love and praise to the Father becomes our sacrifice of praise also, which we offer with him to the Father in the eucharistic sacrifice. The eucharistic sacrifice is, therefore, our great act of worship, cult, and adoration of the Father, with the Son, in the Holy Spirit. It is the perfect sacrifice of the New Testament, which Christians offer to God, with Christ, in the Holy Spirit. It is our sacrifice of praise, love, and the gift of ourselves with Christ to the Father.

Christ came to the earth for our justification, sanctification, illumination, transformation, and divinization. He justifies us by his death in substitution for us. Then we can rise with him in his resurrection to a new life in God. Finally, through the Eucharist, we can continue to grow in holiness through our contact with his eucharistic body that divinizes us, putting us into sacramental and physical contact with the humanity of Jesus Christ, which contains his divinity, to illuminate us from within. In the Eucharist, his divinity illuminates and divinizes our humanity. Thus does God work the salvation and transformation of the world through Jesus Christ.

The Glory of God in Jesus Christ

> "Truly, truly, I say to you, you seek me, not because you saw signs, but because you ate your fill of the loaves. Do not labor for the food which perishes, but for the food which endures to eternal life, which the Son of Man will give you."
> (John 6:26–27)

Jesus complains that this crowd has followed him only because they have eaten of the loaves and filled themselves with bread instead of following him because they had seen divine signs and were seeking God. Jesus, therefore, says that they should instead work "for the food which endures to eternal life," which the Son of Man will give them (John 6:27). They then ask him what they should do to be working for this permanent food. Jesus responds, saying, "This is the work of God, that you believe in him whom he has sent" (John 6:29). In other words, if they want to have this spiritual food, which endures to eternal life, they have to believe in Jesus Christ, whom God has sent for their salvation.

This is the great work they must do—believe in Jesus Christ. But in reality, this is not work but faith. They have to have faith in him because God has sent him to them for their salvation, to give them the bread "which endures to eternal life." And he himself is, moreover, this bread "which comes down from heaven, and gives life to the world" (John 6:33). He himself is this heavenly bread, this bread of life, this living bread, which "gives life to the world" (John 6:33) and which "endures to eternal life." It is for this bread that they are to work, not for the bread which perishes.

Man is made for more than this present life. He is made for more than bread that perishes. Perishable bread is not sufficient for him. "Man shall not live by bread alone, but by every word that proceeds from the mouth of God" (Matt. 4:4). But how many today know this? All their work is for the bread, the food, the necessities of material life, and the pleasures of this world and of this life. The beasts of the field are content with this, but such a life is unworthy of a Christian. We should instead live for God, for his glory, to experience his glory, and to live in it. Moses and Aaron said to the people in the desert of Sinai, "At evening you shall know that it was the Lord who brought you out of the land of Egypt, and in the morning you shall see the glory of the Lord" (Ex. 16:6–7). It is for this glory that we should live. It is for this that the Lord saved Israel and led them out of the land of Egypt. He wanted them to be his own people, to know his laws and his will, to live according to his will and be united with him as their God. And he will reveal to them his glory, and they will see and experience it.

And in the morning, they saw the glory of the Lord when he "gave them bread from heaven" (Ps. 105:40) and "rained down upon them manna to eat, and gave them the grain of heaven. Man ate of the bread of the angels" (Ps. 78:24–25). "And as Aaron spoke to the whole congregation of the people of Israel, they looked toward the desert, and behold, the glory of the Lord appeared in the cloud" (Ex. 16:10). This was the glory of God that Moses and Aaron had predicted, saying, "And in the morning you shall see the glory of the Lord" (Ex. 16:7).

This is the glory that we too yearn for, and we have it in Jesus Christ, who is "the true bread from heaven" (John 6:32), "which comes down from heaven, and gives life to the world" (John 6:33), life which does not perish because he is the bread "which endures to eternal life" (John 6:27). This is the bread for which we are to work; and the work that we are to do to obtain it is to believe in him. "This is the work of God, that you believe in him whom he has sent" (John 6:29).

Through faith, we come into contact with this glory for which we were made. By believing in Jesus Christ, we are remade. Our sins are more than merely pardoned; even their just punishment is paid for us by the suffering of the Lamb of God on the cross. Justice is satisfied. It is not merely a free pardon, a "presidential pardon." Our debt of suffering in punishment for our sins has actually been paid for us by someone, and that someone is no less than the Son of God himself—and he paid for it on the cross and paid for it in full. Therefore divine justice is satisfied, and we are freed to live a new life in the light with Jesus Christ. Our old man is put off in him, and we are now clothed anew with the new man (Eph. 4:22–24; Gal. 3:27; Rom. 13:14). This is the renewal of our minds (Rom. 12:2) and hearts. It is walking in the Spirit and no longer according to the flesh (Rom. 8:5, 13). It is rising with Christ to a new and risen life (Rom. 6:4). Jesus therefore says, "He who comes to me shall not hunger, and he who believes in me shall never thirst" (John 6:35). Jesus Christ is the fountain of this new life. He forgives and renews us. He makes us new men in him (Eph. 4:24), a new creation (2 Cor. 5:17; Gal. 6:15; Rev. 21:5), with renewed minds (Rom. 12:2).

Jesus Christ works in us through his sacraments when we come to him with faith. God justifies us through the death of Jesus Christ when we believe in him and invoke the merits of his death on the cross. He forgives us and cleanses our consciences, giving us a new life. We rise with him in his resurrection (Rom. 6:4) and draw life and glory from him (John 1:16). We live, therefore, henceforth for him, and for him alone with all our hearts. This is the meaning of believing "in him whom he has sent" as "the work of God" (John 6:29). It is believing for the sake of having this new life.

Food for the Journey

"I am the living bread which came down from heaven; if any
one eats of this bread, he will live for ever; and the bread which
I shall give for the life of the world is my flesh."
(John 6:51)

Jesus Christ is "the bread of life" (John 6:48), "the living bread which
came down from heaven" (John 6:51). He is "the bread of life" so that
we might eat of it and live forever. This bread gives us eternal life. "If
any one eats of this bread, he will live for ever" (John 6:51). "This is
the bread which comes down from heaven, that one may eat of it and
not die" (John 6: 50).

This "living bread," this "bread of life," is the great gift that Jesus
Christ has given to us so that we might have divine life in us. Christ
came from God, from the bosom of the Father, to give us the life of
God that does not die so that we might live with God, even now, by
eating this bread; and afterward, in heaven, and then in the world of
the resurrection when Christ comes again in glory with his holy angels
on the clouds of heaven.

This new life in God begins when we believe in Jesus Christ, whose
sacrifice of himself gained all this for us. St. Paul tells us, "Christ loved
us and gave himself up for us, a fragrant offering and sacrifice to God"
(Eph. 5:2). It is this sacrifice of himself that saved us. He perfectly
pleased his Father by his life and his sacrifice of himself on the cross
so that the Father raised him from the dead and poured out his Holy
Spirit upon him and upon all who share with him a human nature if
only they believe in him as their redeemer. His gift of himself in love to
the Father always pleased the Father, as he offered himself in this way
from all eternity; but when he did it this time in human flesh, on the

cross, the result was the salvation of all who share his human nature and believe in him.

Jesus Christ not only infinitely pleased his Father by the loving gift of himself on the cross, but he also bore our sins, and through his suffering, he paid our debt of suffering for our sins so that we would not have to suffer it again.

Then, rising with him in his resurrection to a new life, we are fed by him so that we might live with God's life in us, nevermore to die. It is in this bread of life that we rejoice with gratitude. Since Jesus Christ is God and man, he can let us eat his human body, which he sacramentalized for us in the form of bread. In eating his human body, we eat him, the only Son of God made man. We eat the flesh of God and drink his blood. If God had not become man, he would not have a body that we could eat; but having become man, he can give himself to us to eat. Yet since he is at the same time also God, we not only eat the flesh of a man but also the flesh of God for the life of our spirits.

The Eucharist is our manna. In the morning, we see the glory of God, as the Israelites saw the glory of God in the morning when they discovered the manna that came down with the dew and covered the face of the desert (Exod. 16:13–14). In the morning, we discover this bread from heaven that strengthens our spirits so that we can walk and grow in the life of God. It is like the cake baked on hot stones in the desert, south of Beersheba, where Elijah fled to save his life. He was asleep under a broom tree when an angel woke him and showed him the cake and a jar of water. Twice the angel woke him and said, "Arise and eat." And twice Elijah ate of this heavenly bread "and went in the strength of that food forty days and forty nights to Horeb, the mount of God" (1 Kings 19:8).

The Eucharist is our bread from heaven, our "bread of life," our "living bread," which Jesus Christ gives to those who believe in him and are justified and saved by his sacrifice. He gives us this bread to strengthen us in our new life and to fill us with himself for our divinization and sanctification. With this bread, we continue to offer his one and only sacrifice of himself on the cross to the Father, the perfect sacrifice of the

New Testament, in which is our salvation. It is this sacrifice that propitiated the Father, infinitely pleasing him, thereby winning our salvation. At the same time, this sacrifice also paid our debt of suffering for all our sins so that we could go free, forgiven and saved by our faith in him. Through this sacrifice, we are made resplendent with the light of God in us. It is the source of our new life in God in the light.

The Eucharistic Bread Gives Life to Our Souls

"As the living Father sent me, and I live because of the Father, so he who eats me will live because of me."
(John 6:57)

We are saved through Jesus Christ. He gives us new life. He renews us interiorly, filling us with his own divine life, which is the life of his divine person, contained within a human nature and then sacramentalized in the form of bread and wine. In this way, we can truly eat his flesh and drink his blood and thus have within us the life of God that transforms us. Eating his body unites us to God. It puts God into us, and us into God. Jesus unites us to God because Jesus Christ is in the Father, and the Father is in him by nature, for they share the same nature, the same divine being. But through the eucharistic bread, which we eat, the same Jesus Christ is also in us, and we are in him. Since Jesus is one with the Father, and now, through the Eucharist, is also one with us, he becomes the link that unites us to the Father. Thus by receiving Holy Communion with faith, we are united to the Father. "In that day," said Jesus, "you will know that I am in my Father, and you in me, and I in you" (John 14:20).

It is the death and resurrection of Jesus Christ that saves and justifies us. It is the sacrifice of his death on the cross that infinitely pleased the Father and paid our debt of suffering in punishment for our sins, and for the sin of Adam. And it is in his resurrection that, once we have been forgiven and justified by his death, we rise in him, and with him, to a new and risen life. But in this new and risen life, we grow in sanctity through our union with the Father by means of our union with Jesus Christ. And this union takes place, above all, through the Eucharist.

Through the Eucharist, we live through Jesus Christ, that is, we draw life from him or we live by means of him or from him or because of him, just as he lives through the Father or because of the Father or by means of the Father or from the Father, drawing his life from the Father. Thus we draw life through Jesus Christ. "As the living Father sent me and I live *because* of the Father, so he who eats me will live *because* of me" (John 6:57). This is the way God gave us to have divine life in us. In this way, Jesus Christ gives us new life and shines in our hearts (2 Cor. 4:6). We will live through him. Because he lives, we live. We live because of him. "Yet a little while," Jesus said, "and the world will see me no more, but you will see me; because I live, you will live also" (John 14:19). We live *because* he lives. He is our life. As he lives from his Father, so we live from him. "He who eats me will live *because* of me … as I live *because* of the Father" (John 6:57). We live through Christ or because of Christ by eating his eucharistic flesh, which is his flesh sacramentalized for us in the form of bread. Such is the plan of God to unite man with God. "God sent his only Son into the world, so that we might live *through* him" (1 John 4:9). And we live *through* him by receiving him in Holy Communion.

If we do not receive the Eucharist, we will not have his life in us, and we will not grow in sanctity nor be made new creatures truly justified by Jesus Christ. "Truly, truly, I say to you, if you do not eat the flesh of the Son of Man and drink his blood, you have no life in you" (John 6:53). We are truly made righteous and new and *really* justified—not just *declared* righteous—because we eat the flesh and drink the blood of Jesus Christ. Those who have not had this experience—that is, those who do not receive the Eucharist—do not have the fullness of Christ's life in them, for "if you do not eat the flesh of the Son of Man and drink his blood, you have no life in you" (John 6:53). *True* justification and transformation is dependent upon receiving Christ sacramentally in the Eucharist. This is why the Catholic tradition has always emphasized the *true* nature of our justification, that it is more than just a forensic declaration. It is because in receiving the Eucharist, we experience ourselves as *truly* justified and united to God, divinized by Christ present within us and made *truly* new (Rev. 21:5), a new creation (2 Cor. 5:17), a new creature (Gal. 6:15), a new man (Eph. 4:22–24).

The flesh of Christ is real food, and it gives us the life of God and unites us with God, for it unites us with his Son. "He who eats my flesh and drinks my blood abides in me, and I in him" (John 6:56). So if we want to grow in Christ and in holiness, the means to do so is the Eucharist. "For my flesh is food indeed, and my blood is drink indeed" (John 6:55). And "he who eats my flesh and drinks my blood has eternal life" (John 6:54).

In the eucharistic sacrifice, we offer, with Christ, to the Father, the sacrifice that justifies us. This sacrifice perfectly pleased the Father, for it was the sacrifice in love of his own Son. It also paid our debt of suffering, which we would otherwise have had to pay in punishment for our sins. Then in Holy Communion, we eat the eucharistic Christ so that his divine life might be in us, and we might be truly changed—made truly righteous and sanctified. If we want to grow in Christ, in the life of God and in our union with God, the way to do so is to frequently—even daily—celebrate and receive the Eucharist.

The Eucharist, Food for Our Souls

> "After this many of his disciples drew back and no longer went
> about with him."
> (John 6:66)

Jesus just finished explaining the Eucharist, that is, that his disciples
would eat his flesh and drink his blood. The result of his discourse was
that "after this many of his disciples drew back and no longer went
about with him" (John 6:66). So it also is today. The Eucharist causes
divisions among those who believe in Christ. Not every Christian believes that we really eat Jesus's flesh and drink his blood in the Eucharist.

When I was a child and heard this passage, I always wondered why
Jesus didn't explain this matter more clearly, namely that they were not
to eat his flesh in the way they were imagining, but rather in eucharistic
form, with his flesh sacramentalized in the form of bread; and they were
going to drink his blood sacramentalized in the form of wine.

But I no longer think this way. Do you really think that such an
explanation would have helped them to accept his teaching? Do you
really think that such an explanation would have been easier to believe?
Do you really think that it is easier to believe that Jesus Christ is God,
being his only Son, made man, and that he came to earth in incarnate
form as a man to expiate our sins and to unite us to God by means of his
death, and that he would then rise from the dead so that we that believe
in him might rise with him, made new by him with our sins forgiven?
Would it be easier to believe that he then wanted to feed us spiritually
with his flesh and blood, which contained his divine person and divine
life? Is it easier to believe that he had the power to sacramentalize his real,
human flesh in the form of bread that we could eat, with the result that

we would have God's life physically and sacramentally in us to transform us more and more into Christ, into his image? Truly, I now see that this explanation is far more difficult to believe, understand, and accept than the discourse that he actually gave.

The Eucharist is a difficult doctrine to believe, and many of today's Christians who believe in Jesus Christ for their salvation do not believe that the Eucharist is truly his body and blood. Therefore, when Jesus explained something of this mystery, he lost many disciples. What might he have done in order not to have lost them? If he had not spoken about the Eucharist, he would not have lost these disciples; but Jesus did not choose that course of action. It was necessary to preach the whole truth of God, step by step. It is the same with us, his followers, today. We cannot be silent about the Eucharist for fear of losing disciples, or for fear of offending those who do not believe that the Eucharist is really the body and blood of Christ. So it is unavoidable that we will lose followers, that we will lose those who hear or read our sermons if we speak of the Eucharist. But the truth will win out in the end, and we will be blessed for having given a clear witness to it.

Our salvation from sin is in Jesus Christ. But there is more to the gospel than that. The Eucharist enables us to grow in holiness, in the life of God in our heart. We need this spiritual food. We cannot live and grow in Christ without this sacramental food. "If you do not eat the flesh of the Son of Man and drink his blood, you have no life in you" (John 6:53). But "He who eats my flesh and drinks my blood abides in me, and I in him" (John 6:56). This is what we want. We want him to abide in us, giving us his peace.

Many today are interested in contemplative prayer, an intimate form of prayer without ideas or words, which fills us with divine love and heavenly peace. The Eucharist is a great aid to advance in this type of prayer. We can have our best experiences of contemplative prayer if we practice it immediately after receiving Holy Communion. This has certainly been my experience.

We eat the divinity of Jesus Christ, the Son of God, when we receive Holy Communion. It is a true communion with God in our interior.

It fills us with God. It fills us with his light and peace. It strengthens us for the whole Christian life and for all our work for the Lord. It even makes us want to suffer with and for Christ, to give our lives for him, to sacrifice ourselves in love for him and in his service.

We are regenerated by our faith in Jesus Christ; and the Eucharist is the food of the new man, of the new creation, of the new creature, which we now are. As a newborn baby cannot grow without food, so we that are born again in Jesus Christ cannot grow without the Eucharist.

Part IV:
Authentic Preaching of Salvation in Jesus Christ

True Preachers of Salvation Are Few

"The harvest is plentiful, but the laborers are few; pray therefore the
Lord of the harvest to send out laborers into his harvest."
(Luke 10:2)

Jesus sent out evangelists ahead of himself to work for the harvest of
souls. He tells us that the harvest is plentiful. There are many whom
he wants to call and invite, and therefore he needs many laborers for
his harvest. He wants to invite many to faith in him for their salvation,
yet he is dependent on the laborers available for this ministry, and he
complains that they are few.

People need to hear this invitation to salvation in Jesus Christ. Jesus
therefore sends out his apostles and disciples to preach that sins can be
forgiven and that we can be freed from guilt and live in the freedom of
the children of God (Rom. 8:21). Jesus needs laborers to go out and
preach that we can be made righteous and holy before God through the
merits of the death of his Son on the cross. Such laborers are to preach
repentance, the confessing and leaving behind of sins, and the beginning
of a new life through faith in Christ.

But how many preachers and evangelists preach this message today
and direct people in this way to Jesus Christ? Even among those that
are sent out to preach, how many preach the gospel of God's salvation
in Jesus Christ—that is, that he suffered for the sake of the expiation of
our sins, absorbing into himself, for our sake, the divine wrath against
sin so that we would not have to suffer it? How many of those sent
out clearly preach that "he was wounded for our transgressions ... was
bruised for our iniquities," that "the chastisement of our peace was upon
him," that "with his stripes we are healed," and that "the Lord hath laid
on him the iniquity of us all" (Isa. 53:5–6 KJV)?

How many, even among preachers, preach today that Jesus Christ, the only Son of God, "bore our sins in his body on the tree, that we might die to sin and live to righteousness" (1 Pet. 2:24)? How many preach that Christ suffered what we should have suffered for our sins, becoming a curse for us and in place of us (Gal. 3:13) so that we would not have to suffer this, so we could go free, acquitted, absolved from our sins, and relieved of the burden of our guilt?

Jesus, therefore, says that although the harvest is plentiful, the laborers are few—true preachers of the gospel are few. We are to pray, therefore, that the Lord of the harvest send out laborers into his harvest, true laborers who will not just preach human ideas, or their own ideas, or human philosophy, or tell folksy stories, but actually and powerfully preach the salvation of God in his Son, Jesus Christ, our Lord.

Because it renews the hearts of individuals, this is what will renew the world.

We Now Live in the Messianic Times

"You hypocrites! You know how to interpret the appearance of earth and sky; but why do you not know how to interpret the present time?"
(Luke 12:56)

Jesus tells the Jews that although they know how to predict the weather by interpreting the signs in the clouds and sky, they do not know how to interpret the far more important signs of the present time, in which they are now living, and so they do not recognize that the Messianic times have arrived and that Jesus is their Messiah and Savior. They do not recognize that Jesus is the Son of God, who came to fulfill the Messianic prophecies and bring Israel the salvation it was longing for.

It is good for us too to reflect on these words of Jesus and on the great reality that the Messianic times have arrived—that we now live in these blessed times of salvation. In the Old Testament, the Jews knew Christ in a dark and shadowy way, through signs and symbols, and were awaiting the full and clear revelation of this salvation with the coming of the Messiah. But we have already received this salvation. We have already seen the Messiah, the Savior. We have heard his voice and his teachings and know that he has saved us through his sacrificial death on the cross.

It is this sacrificial death of the only Son of God, the Messiah of Israel, that saves us. This act of Christ changes everything for us. It delivers us from the darkness of sin and error, from the pain of eternal death and from the inner pain of guilt, and puts us into the splendid light of the Lord, with Christ shining in our hearts (2 Cor. 4:6). He illuminates us from within, making us righteous and resplendent before God. This death in sacrifice of the only Son of God re-creates us, making us a new creation (2 Cor. 5:17; Rev. 21:5; Gal. 6:15), new men (Eph. 4:24), clothed with

Jesus Christ (Gal. 3:27; Rom. 13:14), righteous and justified through our faith in him, and resplendent in this world (Matt. 5:14–16; Phil. 2:15). It transforms us "from glory to glory," in the very image of Christ, whose glory we contemplate (2 Cor. 3:18; John 17:22).

Jesus Christ substituted for us on the cross—taking our place, being made a curse for us and in place of us (Gal. 3:13)—so that we might go free from the curse due to our sins, he bearing it instead of us. This is so that we might now be freed from punishment and the pain of guilt to walk in the freedom of the children of God (Rom. 8:21), in the newness of life (Rom. 4:6), in the newness of the Spirit (Rom. 7:6), as new creatures in Jesus Christ (2 Cor. 5:17).

He then rose from the dead to illuminate us with the new light of his resurrection so that we might walk in its splendor. And he ascended to the right hand of the Father, to send us the Holy Spirit from the Father, that we might "walk by the Spirit" (Gal. 5:25), interiorly renewed by the Spirit to live a life in the Spirit, and no longer according to the flesh (Rom. 8:4).

All this comes to us from the cross and resurrection of Jesus Christ. It is therefore of supreme importance to discern well the signs of these Messianic times of salvation in Jesus Christ our Lord, and to preach a clear message of salvation in Jesus Christ.

Transformed into New Creatures by Jesus Christ

"As they were gathering in Galilee, Jesus said to them, The Son of Man is to be delivered into the hands of men, and they will kill him, and he will be raised on the third day. And they were greatly distressed."
(Matt. 17:22–23)

Here Jesus predicts the two most important events of his life, his death and resurrection; in them is our salvation, justification, and new birth in the Spirit to live a new and risen life in him.

Then there follows a discussion about the payment of the temple tax, in which Jesus asks Peter, "'From whom do kings of the earth take toll or tribute? From their sons or from others?' And when he said, 'From others,' Jesus said to him, 'Then the sons are free'" (Matt. 17:25–26). In other words, Jesus and his disciples have no obligation to pay the temple tax because he is the Son of the King of heaven, and his disciples are adopted sons of the King in their brother Jesus.

We are adopted sons of God in Jesus, the only Son of God by nature. He will be put to death and rise from the dead. All who are in him by faith will rise with him to a new life in the Spirit, justified and made holy by their faith in him.

Indeed, we are made resplendent and holy in Christ, filled with light and the love of God to live now, ahead of time, a new and risen life in the risen Christ. Christ's resurrection into glory enables us that believe in him to rise spiritually in glory and walk in the light of Christ. We can rise with Christ because, by believing in him, our sins are absolved through his death, and so we are interiorly renewed. The burden and punishment of our guilt has been lifted from us by Christ himself having become accursed for our sake (Gal. 3:13) and instead of us. We, therefore, are set free.

It is, furthermore, through the sacraments, particularly the sacraments of reconciliation and the Eucharist, regularly received with faith, that all of this comes to be a living experience for us, a true interior renewal by the Holy Spirit. Sin is removed from our consciences and we are freed from guilt and filled with new life through receiving these sacraments. This is why Christ's justification and salvation is, for us, something real and experiential, not merely forensic. It makes us truly new and righteous in God's sight, truly transforming us into new creatures, new men, a new creation in Jesus Christ, our Lord.

Bibliography

Beilby, James, and Paul R. Eddy, eds. *The Nature of the Atonement: Four Views.* Downers Grove, IL: IVP Academic, 2006.

Berkhof, Louis. *Systematic Theology.* Grand Rapids: Eerdmans, 1938, rpt. 1996.

Bridges, Jerry, and Bob Bevington. *The Great Exchange: My Sin for His Righteousness.* Wheaton, IL: Crossway, 2007.

Calvin, John. *Institutes of the Christian Religion.* Tr. Henry Beveridge. Grand Rapids: Eerdmans, rpt. 1989.

Denney, James. *The Death of Christ: Its Place and Interpretation in the New Testament.* New York: A. C. Armstrong and Son, 1904.

Finlan, Stephen, and Vladimir Kharlamov. *Theosis: Deification in Christian Theology.* Princeton Theological Monograph Series. Eugene, Oregon: Pickwick, 2006.

Grenz, Stanley J. *Rediscovering the Triune God: The Trinity in Contemporary Theology.* Minneapolis: Fortress, 2004.

Gross, Jules. *The Divinization of the Christian According to the Greek Fathers.* Anaheim, CA: A & C, rpt. 2002.

Haldane, Robert. *Exposition of Romans*. Lafayette, IN: Sovereign Grace, rpt. 2001.

Hodge, Charles. *Commentary on the Epistle to the Romans*. Grand Rapids: Eerdmans, rpt. 1994.

———. *Systematic Theology*. 3 vols. Grand Rapids: Eerdmans, rpt. 1997.

Jeffery, Steve, Michael Ovey, and Andrew Sach. *Pierced for Our Transgressions: Rediscovering the Glory of Penal Substitution*. Wheaton, IL: Crossway, 2007.

Kärkkäinen, Veli-Matti. *One with God: Salvation as Deification and Justification*. Collegeville, MN: Liturgical, 2004.

———. *The Trinity: Global Perspectives*. Louisville: Westminster John Knox, 2007.

Kasper, Walter. *The God of Jesus Christ*. New York: Crossroads, 1986.

Lloyd-Jones, D. Martyn. *Romans: An Exposition of Chapters 3:20–4:25 Atonement and Justification*. Edinburgh: Banner of Truth Trust, rpt. 2007.

———. *The Cross: God's Way of Salvation*. Wheaton: Crossway, 1986.

Mannermaa, Tuomo. *Christ Present in Faith: Luther's View of Justification*. Minneapolis: Fortress, 2005.

Moo, Douglas J. *The Epistle to the Romans*. New International Commentary on the New Testament. Grand Rapids: Eerdmans, 1996.

Morris, Leon. *The Apostolic Preaching of the Cross*. Grand Rapids: Eerdmans, rpt. 1965.

————. *The Atonement: Its Meaning and Significance*. Downers Grove, IL: IVP Academic, 1983.

Packer, J. I., and Mark Dever. *In My Place Condemned He Stood: Celebrating the Glory of the Atonement*. Wheaton, IL: Crossway, 2007.

Reymond, Robert L. *A New Systematic Theology of the Christian Faith*. 2nd ed. Revised. Nashville: Thomas Nelson, 1997.

Russell, Norman. *The Doctrine of Deification in the Greek Patristic Tradition*. Oxford Early Christian Studies. Clarendon, Oxford: Oxford University Press, 2004.

Schreiner, Thomas R. *Romans*. Baker Exegetical Commentary on the New Testament. Grand Rapids: Baker Academic, 1998.

Stott, John R. *The Cross of Christ*. Downers Grove, IL: IVP Books, 1986, rpt. 2006.

Tidball, Derek, David Hilborn, and Justin Thacker, eds. *The Atonement Debate: Papers from the London Symposium on the Theology of Atonement*. Grand Rapids: Zondervan, 2008.

Ware, Bruce. *Father, Son, and Holy Spirit: Relationships, Roles, and Relevance*. Wheaton, IL: Crossway, 2005.